T0330238

Modelling Corporation Tax Revenue

Modelling Corporation Tax Revenue

John Creedy

The Truby Williams Professor of Economics, University of Melbourne, Australia

Norman Gemmell

Chief Economist, The Treasury, New Zealand

Edward Elgar
Cheltenham, UK • Northampton, MA, USA

Published by
Edward Elgar Publishing Limited
The Lypiatts
15 Lansdown Road
Cheltenham
Glos GL50 2JA
UK

Edward Elgar Publishing, Inc.
William Pratt House
9 Dewey Court
Northampton
Massachusetts 01060
USA

A catalogue record for this book
is available from the British Library

Library of Congress Control Number: 2010925969

ISBN 978 1 84844 765 3

Printed and bound by MPG Books Group, UK

Contents

I Introduction

II Corporate Profits and Tax Revenue

III   A Simulation Model

IV   Corporate Tax Simulations

V   Conclusions

List of Figures

List of Tables

Acknowledgements

This book makes substantial use of a number of journal articles, though they have been considerably revised and rearranged. These are Creedy and Gemmell (2008, 2009, 2010a, 2010b, 2010c). We are grateful to the editors and publishers for permission to use the material here. This research was started while Norman Gemmell was at Her Majesty's Revenue and Customs (HMRC) Analysis department. We are grateful to colleagues there for their support, especially David Ulph and Edwin Ko. The views expressed here are those of the authors and do not necessarily reflect those of HMRC. Further research was conducted while Norman Gemmell was visiting the Centre for Business Taxation, Oxford University. We are grateful to colleagues there for their support, especially the director, Mike Devereux. The research was also facilitated by visits by John Creedy to Nottingham University and the Oxford Centre for Business Taxation during April and May 2007, and several visits to the New Zealand Treasury and the Institute for the Study of Competition and Regulation (ISCR) and the Centre for Accounting, Governance and Taxation Research (CAGTR), in the School of Accounting and Commercial Law at the Victoria University of Wellington.

Part I

Introduction

Chapter 1

Introduction and Outline

The economic analysis of corporate taxation has traditionally been something of a 'poor relation' of taxation analysis, although interest in this topic has been expanding in more recent years.[1] To a large extent the expanding body of modern research on corporate income taxes reflects a growing recognition that understanding those corporate tax issues which were of traditional interest in the context of closed economies – such as corporate tax incidence or the response of company investment to taxation – are increasingly important as globalisation means that open economy aspects must be analysed explicitly. Nevertheless, revenue aspects of corporate income taxes have remained relatively under-explored. In particular, though the tax revenue growth properties of income taxes have been extensively studied, there has been little analysis undertaken of the revenue growth properties of corporate income taxes. This book begins

---

[1]For example, in the *Handbook of Public Economics* series, published by Elsevier, neither of the first two volumes (1985 and 1987) includes a chapter on corporate taxation, and the term does not appear in the Index. Volumes 3 and 4, published in 2002, acknowledge the increasing interest in, and analysis of, the topic by including a chapter by Auerbach (2002) on 'Taxation and Corporate Financial Policy', and by examining the role of tax policy in business investment decisions, and international taxation, much of which relates to multinational corporations.

to address this deficiency. It provides in many ways a companion volume to Creedy and Gemmell (2006) which examined the revenue growth properties of income and consumption taxes.

This chapter begins, in section 1.1, by outlining some of the reasons why an examination of the revenue properties of corporate income taxes is important. Section 1.2 then discusses the concepts of tax buoyancy and fiscal drag – or 'built-in flexibility' – as applied to corporate taxation, examining revenue and profit movements in the UK. The emphasis of the book is on the characteristics and determinants of the corporation tax 'revenue elasticity' – the proportional change in corporate tax revenues in association with a proportional change in the tax base (profits) holding other factors constant. It will be seen that the special nature of corporate profits, compared with individual incomes, and the associated tax structure, present substantial modelling challenges compared with the personal income tax system. After introducing the buoyancy and elasticity concepts, section 1.3 provides a brief outline of future chapters.

1.1   Corporate Tax Revenue

The rationale for a corporate income tax, as distinct from income taxes on individuals has been extensively debated in the tax literature and is not examined in this book. But, given the widespread use of corporate income taxes across OECD and other countries, it is clearly important to understand those influences on revenue-raising and other properties of the tax. As with any tax, a key consideration for corporate income taxes is how to raise a given amount of revenue at minimum efficiency cost. Modelling corporate tax revenue in particular is important for a number of reasons.

First, any analysis of the social welfare impacts of a tax needs first to identify the economic, as distinct from legal, incidence of that tax. With corporation tax the incidence on individuals' and households' welfare is indirect, being mediated through impacts of profit taxation on output prices and wages. For this reason corporate tax incidence is especially difficult to identify empirically. The quantitative significance of these incidence problems become greater, the larger the amount of revenue governments seek to raise from corporate taxation. Similarly, revenue and incidence are influenced by the nature of the corporate tax regime, such as the extent of profit distribution to company shareholders, the use of imputation systems, and the extent and type of exemptions from the corporate tax regime (such as interest deductions and the rate structure).

Second, behaviour responses to corporate taxes – both by corporations themselves and by those shareholders and workers on whom the tax is incident – determine how much revenue a given corporate tax structure raises. These responses are examined in more detail is subsequent chapters. The recent literature has recognised that they can take a number of forms. These include: changes in corporate structure; investment choices, both locational and marginal; financial arrangements; transfer pricing and the location of declared corporate profits, deductions, and corporate headquarters. A suitable model of corporate income tax revenue needs to recognise and measure these responses as accurately as possible.

Third, the modelling of corporate tax revenue is important for tax revenue forecasting especially, as is shown in subsequent chapters, because corporate tax revenue appear to be highly sensitive to the short-run fluctuations associated with economic cycles. Corporate income taxes are known to be among the most volatile of taxes typically collected by OECD governments. This reflects, in part, the fact that the corporate tax base, company profit, is generally more volatile than other tax bases such as those based on personal incomes or expenditure. The volatility also reflects, as subsequent chapters show, the way in which most corporate tax regimes treat profits differently between when they are positive and when they are negative (that is, when losses are made).

Fourth, globalisation is generating increased international capital mobility such that the setting of tax rates on capital in general, and corporate profits in particular, increasingly needs to take account of responses to those tax rates both 'at home' and abroad. This is sometimes claimed to be responsible, in part at least, for the so-called 'race to the bottom' in international corporate tax rates. For example, Devereux *et al.* (2008) have investigated how far OECD countries compete with each other in setting corporate tax rates, and whether this competition can explain the observed declines in statutory tax rates since the early 1980s. They find evidence of what they refer to as 'strategic interaction' between governments over the setting of corporate statutory rates, but only for open economies (those without capital controls on international investment flows). They also show that 'equilibrium' statutory rates fell substantially over recent decades and similarly to those observed empirically. Their conclusion is that the 'reductions in equilibrium tax rates can be explained almost entirely by more intense competition generated by the relaxation of capital controls' (2008, p. 1210).

National corporate tax revenue in open economies therefore

appears increasingly to be vulnerable to international changes in statutory corporate tax rates and other aspects of corporate tax regimes, such as deductions claiming, as evidence discussed in later chapters shows. For tax authorities seeking to funding existing public spending levels, this raises the important issue of how far other tax rates may have to be raised to compensate for 'lost' corporate revenue, either because the corporate rate has to be lowered to be competitive or because, with an unchanged corporate tax rate, the tax base shifts to other countries. If this 'lost revenue' has to be raised from taxes with more or different distortionary impacts, then assessing the consequences of possible corporate revenue changes becomes especially important.

Recent trends in OECD corporate tax rates are shown in Figure 1.1, from Devereux (2008), which shows that there has been a persistent downward trend in OECD countries' corporate tax rates since at least the early 1980s, with a median rate around 50 per cent in 1982, but around 35 per cent by 2004. Whether this trend continues in future may depend on countries' reactions to the increased public indebtedness in some major OECD countries that has followed the global recession of 2008–10.

Countries such as the US, Ireland and the UK that have experienced large increases in public debt may be reluctant to pursue further corporate tax rate reductions. On the other hand, competition from countries with less public debt overhang problems may be able to continue sustainable reductions in corporate tax rates, so putting pressure on the more indebted countries to raise any additional revenues via other taxes.

Though statutory corporate tax rates are arguably the most relevant tax variable affecting profit-shifting decisions by multinational companies (see Devereux and Sorensen, 2005), the ef-

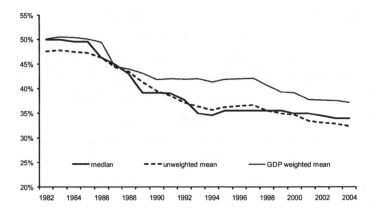

Figure 1.1: OECD Statutory Corporation Tax Rates 1982–2004

fective average tax rates (EATRs) and effective marginal tax rates (EMTRs) are more relevant to investment location and expansion or contraction aspects. These tax rates have also been declining in recent decades. Table 1.1 shows changes in EATRs, for example, for several OECD countries between 1982 and 2004. With the exception of Ireland (already low by 1982) these fall over the period to greater or lesser degrees. In general the highest rates in 1982 tended to fall the most.

The overall revenue impact of changes in statutory or effective rates depends on both any base broadening measures that are undertaken, such as restrictions to depreciation allowances and any behavioural responses to those tax parameter changes; see Devereux and Sorensen (2005). Figure 1.2, from Devereux (2008), shows how corporate tax revenue has moved as a percentage of GDP since the mid-1960s in OECD countries on average. Of particular interest here is the tendency since the early 1980s for corporate tax revenue to increase (except for the GDP-

Table 1.1: OECD Effective Average Tax Rates 1982 and 2004 (percentages)

Country	1982	2004
Australia	37	26
Austria	37	24
Belgium	35	26
Canada	25	28
Finland	45	23
France	34	27
Germany	48	32
Greece	36	23
Ireland	5	11
Italy	26	26
Japan	44	32
Netherlands	38	28
Norway	38	24
Portugal	48	20
Spain	26	26
Sweden	45	21
Switzerland	26	25
UK	26	24
USA	32	25

weighted case where large economies such as the US dominate), despite the general decline in statutory rates.

This general trend growth in revenue, notwithstanding cyclical fluctuations, suggests that corporate tax regimes are becoming more, not less, important sources of government revenue to finance their expenditure programmes. It also suggests that understanding the drivers of behavioural responses to corporate tax rate and other parameter changes may be important for understanding how revenue can be expected to move in response to future tax rate changes.

Finally, the global recession in 2008–10 has demonstrated the potential volatility of corporate tax revenues over the short term.

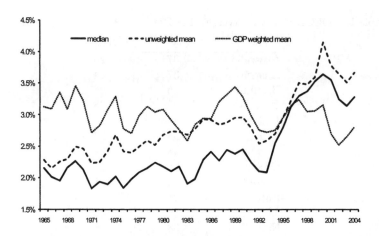

Figure 1.2: OECD Corporation Tax Revenue as a Percentage of GDP 1965–2004

It has been found that this phenomenon can affect the corporate tax receipts of different countries in very different ways. The most obvious cases of dramatic short-term impacts include Ireland, with its heavy reliance on overseas (mainly US and EU) multinationals, and the UK and US, which both experienced relatively severe banking sector crises and have corporate tax regimes that rely relatively heavily on the financial sector – both domestically-owned and foreign-owned.

The importance of this recession-related volatility, and the difficulties of forecasting it, are seen clearly in the Irish and UK cases in Tables 1.2 and 1.3 respectively. Table 1.2 shows that, for Ireland, an estimated corporate tax receipts total of €6,000 for 2008 was expected to continue at around that level (€5,950) for 2009 at the time of the 2009 Budget in October 2008.[2] Within six months however this estimate had been cut

---

[2]These   data   are   taken   from   *Government   of   Ireland,   Department*

to €3,740 for 2009, and by Budget 2010 (in December 2009), projected receipts for 2010 were further reduced to €3,210. In other words, the global recession had both a devastating effect on corporate tax receipts and on the ability to forecast these over the short term. Receipts in 2009 look likely to be around only 60 per cent of their 2008 level with a further fall to around 54 per cent expected in 2010. These are very large short-term changes by any standards.

Table 1.2: Corporate Tax Receipts, Ireland 2008-2011: €Millions

	2008 Estimated outturn	2009 Estimate	2010 Projection	2011 Projection
Estimate made at:				
Budget 2009:				
(14 October 2008)	6,000	5,950	5,710	6,240
Budget 2009:				
(7 April 2009)		3,740	3,840	4,325
Budget 2010:				
(9 December 2009)		3,790	3,210	

The UK situation is rather different from Ireland, as seen in Table 1.3.[3] The UK corporate tax receipts are especially sensitive to the country's large financial sector, and the country's banking crisis in 2008–09 both immediately reduced that sector's corporate tax payments and raised required tax revenues in the future to pay for the government's bail-out of failing or vulnerable banks such as Northern Rock and the Royal Bank of Scotland.

The impact on corporate tax receipts can be seen in Table 1.3 which records the outturns, estimates and projections of receipts

---

of Finance, *Budget 2009, 2009 Supplementary, 2010,* available at: www.budget.gov.ie/Budgets/2010/2010.aspx.
    [3]These data are from H. Treasury *Pre-Budget Reports, 2006–2009,* available at: www.hm-treasury.gov.uk/prebud_pbr09_index.htm.

Table 1.3: Corporate Tax Receipts, UK 2006/07-2010/11 : £Billions

	2005/06	2006/07	2007/08	2008/09	2009/10	2010/11
Estimate at:	o = outturn; e = estimate; p = projected					
PBR 2006	42.4^o	48.0^e	53.8^p			
PBR 2007		44.8^o	46.8^e	51.5^p		
PBR 2008			46.9^o	45.5^e	42.4^p	
PBR 2009				43.7^o	34.1^e	40.9^p

at the time of the Pre-Budget Reports (PBRs) in 2006–09, usually announced between October and December of each year. Whereas in 2006 it was expected that corporate tax receipts would rise by around 27 per cent from £42.4 billion 2005/06 to £53.8 billion in 2007/08, the 2009 PBR suggests that the outcome was only around 10 per cent growth (to £46.9 billion 2007/08) with a substantial fall to £34.1 billion estimated for 2009/10. Apparently, however, a rapid recovery to £40.9 billion 2010/11 is still projected though the PBR 2009 (p.182) nevertheless notes that, under current forecasts: 'this leaves corporation tax from the [non-North Sea] sector below its 2007–08 level, even by 2014–15'.

As in the Irish case, these are dramatic short-term reductions in corporate tax receipts such that understanding the likely determinants of these changes is clearly important for tax policy. The timing and magnitude of the global banking crisis and subsequent recession might not have been easily predicted or calibrated, but once potential changes in the corporate tax base can be identified or forecast, accurately predicting corporate tax revenues can be enhanced by suitable models capable of capturing the key determinants of these processes. This book offers some insight into the short-term volatility of corporate tax revenues at a time when understanding this volatility is especially pertinent for many governments' tax policy settings.

The data illustrated above in Figure 1.2 for the OECD capture the observed movement of tax revenues with respect to GDP (other 'anchors', such as the relevant tax base, are sometimes used as alternatives). This is commonly referred to as tax buoyancy. To understand the contribution of the corporate tax structure and abstract from other factors that influence revenue growth, such as behavioural responses, changes in compliance and so on, it is usual to examine the built-in flexibility or fiscal drag of the tax. The next section defines these concepts more precisely and highlights recent UK evidence.

1.2 Tax Buoyancy and Fiscal Drag

This section examines, using UK data, variations in taxes and profits over time. This helps to highlight some important empirical features which motivate further detailed analyses of the corporation tax system. Furthermore, it emphasises the need to distinguish between the two different concepts of tax buoyancy and fiscal drag. The former, tax buoyancy, is measured simply by the proportional change, from year to year, in total corporation tax revenue divided by the proportional change in total profits over the period: it therefore has the properties of an elasticity. In practice, changes in revenue are influenced by, among other things, changes in the corporation tax regime itself over the period. The concept of fiscal drag refers on the other hand to the variation in tax revenue which arises purely with an unchanged tax structure as profits vary; that is, the tax rates, thresholds and regulations concerning eligible deductions are held constant. Fiscal drag is therefore often referred to as the built-in flexibility of the tax system, and is measured by the revenue elasticity, defined as the proportional change in tax revenue divided by the proportional change in profits. If the tax paid is a fixed proportion of gross profits, taxes and profits increase in the same proportion and the elasticity is unity. Any tax structure having an increasing average tax rate as profits increase displays a revenue elasticity of greater than unity.

A feature of aggregate corporation tax revenue is that it varies substantially from year to year. This raises the question of whether the variability arises from variations in the relationship between profits and taxes or whether profits themselves are variable, particularly in relation to GDP growth. The vast majority of corporation tax is paid at a fixed marginal rate. It may therefore initially be thought that tax revenue simply increases in proportion to total corporate profits, suggesting that the revenue elasticity is unity and that variability in revenue arises fundamentally from profit variations linked to GDP growth along with actual changes in the corporation tax regime. However, it will be seen that this is far from being the case – the revenue elasticity of corporation taxes is indeed capable of significant variations and of displaying values substantially different from unity.

1.2.1 Corporation Tax Buoyancy in the UK

Corporation tax revenues can be measured either in cash or accrual terms. The former measures the amount of tax paid by companies and received by the UK Revenue and Customs department (HMRC) in a given period, while the latter measures the corporation tax liability as assessed using the tax code during a given period (usually a fiscal year).

Using HMRC data on corporation tax accruals and profits, available on a consistent basis from 1992/93, Figure 1.3 shows the growth rates of tax accrual, dT/T, and gross taxable profits, dP/P, compared to GDP growth, d(GDP)/GDP. These HMRC profit data relate only to company profit as declared for tax purposes and therefore treats all company gross losses as zero profits. They are therefore quite different from profits in companies' commercial accounts which include both positive profits and losses. This demonstrates the much greater variability in gross profit growth compared with GDP growth rates. Furthermore, although both corporation tax accruals and profits are relatively volatile, their growth rates follow quite different patterns. This latter feature contributes substantially to highly volatile corporation tax buoyancy in Figure 1.4.

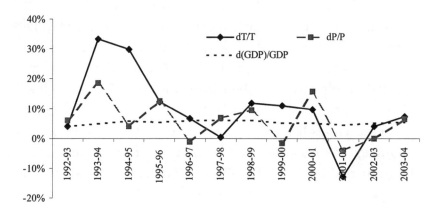

Figure 1.3: Corporation Tax, Profit and GDP Growth Rates

Tax buoyancy is measured as the growth in tax revenue (receipts or accruals) divided by the growth in profits or GDP.

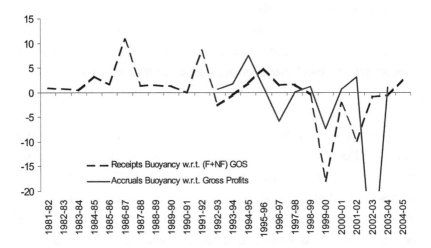

Figure 1.4: Corporation Tax Buoyancy

Figure 1.4 shows the accruals-based buoyancy measure, with respect to GDP and profits, and compares this with a receipts-based measure. The accruals-based measure of profits used here is the HMRC measure of gross taxable trading profits and other taxable income and net capital gains.[4] Corporation tax accruals are derived directly from the HMRC measure of gross profits liable to UK tax, so this provides a more consistent denominator for the accruals-based buoyancy measure from 1992/93. The buoyancy of corporation tax receipts can be examined over a longer period by using the Office of National Statistics measure of profits – the gross operating surplus of financial and non-financial companies, denoted F+NF GOS. This is also shown in Figure 1.4. Constructing receipts buoyancy measures using economy-wide gross operating surplus, GOS, yields similar

---

[4]See http://www.hmrc.gov.uk/stats/corporate_tax/table11_2.pdf. Corporate tax accrual is also available from this source.

evidence of volatility though peaks and troughs often do not coincide. Economy-wide GOS includes F+NF GOS as well as the gross operating surplus of households, non-profit institutions (serving households) and general government.

It can be seen that accrual buoyancy with respect to GDP varies approximately within the range −5 to +5, where +5 implies that tax grew five times as fast as GDP. However, negative buoyancy values can arise either because GDP growth is negative or because tax growth is negative, but not both. If both are negative, a positive buoyancy value results. Receipts and accruals buoyancy can be seen to be quite different, at least on an annual basis. This reflects the different profit series used in the denominator of each measure and the impact of timing differences between corporation tax receipts and accruals.[5] The large negative values arise in years of negative profit growth which are not sufficiently large or sustained to produce negative tax growth. However, unusually large negative profit growth of almost −4 per cent in 2001–02 led to a fall in tax accruals for that year such that accruals buoyancy remained positive. Large positive or negative buoyancy values tend to arise when annual GDP or profit growth is close to zero, so that the small denominator generates a high buoyancy value.

The tax buoyancy observed in Figure 1.4 could result from a number of factors. First, the built-in flexibility, or fiscal drag, properties of the tax structure generate automatic changes in revenues as the tax base changes. Second, revenue can be af-

---

[5]Corporation tax in the UK can be paid either in advance or in arrears of a company's assessed liability. Hence, tax receipts and accruals rarely match exactly in a given fiscal year and can sometimes vary markedly. For example, in 1999 when the Quarterly Instalment Payment (QIPs) system was introduced, receipts exceeded accruals by around 25 per cent as both current and some future liabilities had to be paid.

fected by discretionary changes in tax rates or other tax parameters. Third, changes in revenue can be influenced by changes in compliance effort or efficiency of collection. Although there have been numerous discretionary changes to the corporation tax regime in the UK over the period examined here, and possibly changes in corporation tax compliance of unknown magnitude, it would be surprising if these factors could substantially account for the observed volatility in corporation tax buoyancy. This raises the question of whether fiscal drag, as captured by the tax revenue elasticity, can explain the observed buoyancy volatility.

1.2.2   Fiscal Drag and Revenue Elasticity

Fiscal drag is a familiar feature of income taxes where the existence of fixed or income-related tax allowances, and rising marginal tax rates generate a rising share of total income paid in income tax as average incomes rise. Fiscal drag is therefore a common feature of progressive taxes. It can be measured in unit-free terms by the revenue elasticity of a tax – the automatic percentage increase in tax revenue divided by the percentage increase in the tax base. For progressive taxes this elasticity exceeds one, as revenue rises proportionately faster than the tax base.

Despite numerous studies of the fiscal drag properties of personal income and, to a lesser extent, indirect taxes, there is very little existing analysis of corporation tax fiscal drag. For surveys of, and contributions to, the literature on fiscal drag of income and indirect taxes, see Creedy and Gemmell (2006) and Heinemann (2001). This may reflect, in part, a view that there is less normative significance to a tax that leads to companies with larger profits paying proportionately more tax, compared to a tax where individuals or households with higher personal incomes pay proportionately more tax. Furthermore, where most corporation tax revenue is paid by companies at a single rate, fiscal drag is often presumed to be of little quantitative significance.

In the UK, there are two non-zero corporation tax rates of 19 per cent and 30 per cent: this simple summary conceals the complexity of the structure, which is described in more detail in Chapter 2. However, the lower, 'small company rate' of 19 per cent is levied on companies with net taxable profits (that is, profits after all deductions) below £1.5 million. Even this value exaggerates the importance of the 19 per cent rate since, for companies in groups, the £1.5 million threshold is split between all the companies in the group. It therefore contributes only a small fraction of total revenue raised, the remainder being collected at the 30 per cent rate. Increasing company profits, which push companies across the net profit threshold when they begin to pay tax at the 30 per cent rate, are therefore unlikely to be an important contributor to the overall fiscal drag properties of the UK corporation tax system.

However, UK corporation tax has two features which could contribute importantly to fiscal drag. First, various deductions, allowable against profits or in the form of tax credits, mean that about 60 per cent of gross profit declared for tax purposes is tax-free. Thus for a typical company, the marginal tax rate on profit is higher than its average tax rate. This generates fiscal drag. Second, profits either before or after deductions can be negative, but negative profits (losses) are not eligible for a tax refund. Though various deductions (for example, group relief) provide a form of tax refund on some losses, this is not sufficient to ensure that the effective refund on a given loss is equal to the effective tax on an equivalent amount of profit. The following chapter provides a more detailed analysis of the tax structure and determinants of individual and aggregate revenue elasticities.

This section has used terms such as profits, deductions and tax base without defining them precisely. In the remainder of this book, the corporation tax base is defined as gross (taxable) profits; that is gross profits defined for tax purposes – total profits declared to HMRC as potentially liable to corporation tax. This is distinct from the accounting definition of gross profits where some items of income or expenditure in company accounts are treated differently (for example, interest payments and capital expenditure). Net (taxable) profits are gross (taxable) profits minus all deductions, where deductions are defined as all tax allowances claimed in the form of profit offsets (for example, capital allowances) plus the profit offset equivalents of tax credits (for example, double taxation relief). Corporation tax liability is therefore obtained by multiplying the relevant corporation tax rate by net profits.

1.3   Outline of the Book

The remaining substantive chapters of this book are divided into three Parts. Part II is largely concerned with theoretical aspects. It begins in chapter 2 by looking closely at the corporation tax structure in the UK and examining the likely implications for the revenue elasticity of individual corporations and in aggregate.

A fundamental feature of the income obtained by corporations, unlike that of individuals, is that it can be negative; that is, corporations can and indeed many do make losses. In dealing with positive and negative profits, the tax structure is asymmetric, in that while positive net or taxable profits (defined as gross profits less eligible deductions) are taxed, no rebate is available in respect of losses. However, past losses can be used to some extent to offset current profits. This means that the examination of corporation tax revenue cannot escape a detailed treatment of dynamic aspects. Chapter 3 concentrates on the implications of this asymmetry, particularly for the responses of firms to taxation. Such responses, in the form of income shifting, are examined in further detail in chapter 4. The greater ability to shift activities to other tax juristictions or to shift profits overseas, through the use of transfer pricing, is yet another characteristic of corporations that distinguishes them from individual taxpayers, and thus requires careful consideration. Special attention is given in each chapter to the potential and likely characteristics over the business cycle, where variations involve some firms moving between losses and positive profits.

Further analysis requires the construction of a dynamic simulation model, and this is described in Part III. A central feature of the model, referred to as CorpSim, is the generation of a distribution of firms and their profits, along with the dynamics of profit changes over time. This is complicated by the fact that few data are available, contrasting with the situation facing studies of personal incomes. A further feature of corporation taxes, which no longer exists for personal income taxes, is the division of profits into schedules relating to different sources of corporate income. Hence the model must be capable of generating a joint distribution of profit sources for each firm, along with their time profile over the business cycle. This component of the model is described in chapter 5. The second chapter in Part III, chapter 6, describes the modelling of the use by firms of capital allowances and losses in generating deductions. Again, this presents a special challenge in the case of corporation taxes compared with personal income taxes, where relatively few deductions are available. In particular, firms are able to form groups for tax purposes, whereby losses in one firm can be used – under certain conditions – to offset profits in another firm in the group. Chapter 6 describes an algorithm, or more precisely a series of algorithms, used to compute net or taxable profits for single firms and for firms within groups in such a way that their tax payments are minimised.

Part IV then uses the simulation model, CorpSim, to examine profits and taxes over hypothetical business cycles. Chapter 7 considers the revenue elasticity, while chapter 8 examines profit-shifting responses to tax changes.

1.4 Conclusions

This chapter began by reviewing recent changes in corporation tax rates and revenues. It was suggested that, despite systematic reductions in rates, corporation taxation has become a relatively more important source of revenue for many countries. Special attention was then given to the buoyancy of corporation tax receipts and accruals in the UK in recent years. Buoyancy measures the growth in revenues as a ratio of the growth in profits, or GDP. This ratio is highly volatile from year to year. The chapter then considered whether such volatility could be a feature of the inherent or fiscal drag properties of the UK's corporation tax system. To measure fiscal drag – describing the way tax revenues grow relative to profits for an unchanged tax regime – the tax revenue elasticity measure is used.

The volatility has serious implications for attempts to forecast corporation tax revenue. Experience has shown that corporation taxes are among the most difficult to forecast, using conventional methods based, for example, on regressions of taxes and profits over time. Such regressions, using lag structures and observations over a long time period, may be able to approximate the long-run buoyancy of corporation taxes, and limited cyclical aspects. For example, applying the tax and profit data used in Figure 1.4 to a simple log-log regression of tax revenue on profits, over the period 1978–2004, produces a long-run buoyancy parameter (the coefficient on log profits) of 1.1. With cyclical volatility, such parameter estimates can depend, of course, on the start/end date. An equivalent regression over 1984–2004 yields a parameter of 0.92. However their inability to capture discretionary tax changes mean they cannot distinguish the *ceteris paribus* effects of the revenue elasticity.

This variability suggests that further analysis requires a more detailed treatment of the characteristics of the corporation tax structure and variations in profits and taxes over time, particularly over the business cycle.

Part II

Corporate Profits and Tax Revenue

Chapter 2

The Revenue Elasticity

This chapter examines the basic characteristics of the corporate tax revenue elasticity as it applies to an individual company and all companies combined. Section 2.1 introduces the revenue elasticity in the context of a single company. The role played by deductions is considered further in Section 2.2. Section 2.3 examines the corporation tax schedule and revenue elasticities. Section 2.4 considers aggregation over all firms.

2.1 Revenue Elasticity for Individual Companies

Consider a single company. Gross profits are P and total deductions are D, so that net profits, P^T, are:

$$P^T = P - D \qquad (2.1)$$

Suppose, for simplicity, that there is a single tax rate of t. Hence when $P^T > 0$, the tax liability, $T(P)$, is:

$$T(P) = t(P - D) \qquad (2.2)$$

and when $P^T \leq 0$, $T(P) = 0$. The tax revenue elasticity, $\eta_{T,P}$, for the company is defined as the proportional increase in tax

27

divided by the proportional increase in gross profits, so that:

$$\eta_{T,P} = \frac{dT/T}{dP/P} = \frac{dT}{dP}\frac{P}{T} \qquad (2.3)$$

The elasticity is thus the ratio of the marginal to the average tax rate. From (2.2), the average tax rate, ATR, is given by:

$$ATR = \frac{T(P)}{P} = \frac{t(P-D)}{P} \qquad (2.4)$$

while the marginal tax rate, MTR, is:

$$MTR = \frac{dT(P)}{dP} = t\left(1 - \frac{dD}{dP}\right) = t\left(1 - \frac{D}{P}\eta_{D,P}\right) \qquad (2.5)$$

where $\eta_{D,P}$ is the elasticity of deductions with respect to gross profits. Hence it follows that:

$$\begin{aligned}
\eta_{T,P} &= \frac{1 - \frac{D}{P}\eta_{D,P}}{1 - \frac{D}{P}} \\
&= \left(1 - \frac{dD}{dP}\right)\left(\frac{P}{P-D}\right) \qquad (2.6)
\end{aligned}$$

Equation (2.6) shows that, for a taxpaying company (for which $P - D > 0$), the second term in brackets exceeds unity if $D > 0$, but since $dD/dP0$, the first term is ambiguously signed. Thus the size and sign of both the *level* of deductions relative to net or gross profits, D/P (recalling that $P = P^T + D$), and the *change in* deductions relative to gross profits, dD/dP, are crucial determinants of the revenue elasticity. If deductions are independent of gross profits, then $\eta_{D,P} = 0$, and the revenue elasticity takes the simpler form:

$$\eta_{T,P} = \frac{P}{P-D} \qquad (2.7)$$

In this case the revenue elasticity is simply the ratio of gross to net taxable profit. For companies with positive but very low tax liabilities, that is $P - D$ is small, the elasticity is large, and higher profits reduce the elasticity towards unity. For companies with a zero tax liability (that is, where $P - D \leq 0$), the revenue elasticity is zero.

Figure 2.1 illustrates this case. The profile, WXX'Y, shows the revenue elasticity as profit increases. Along the range WX, profit increases from zero or negative values towards $P = D$, and the elasticity remains zero. At $P = D$ the elasticity becomes infinitely large because the denominator in equation (2.7) is zero. Beyond this point, over the range X'Y, the elasticity declines asymptotically towards unity as P increases further.

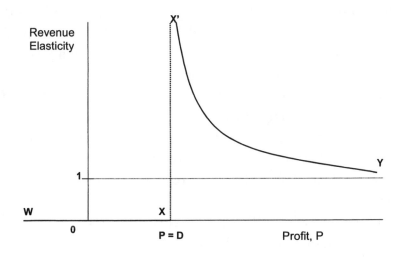

Figure 2.1: Individual Revenue Elasticity

2.2   Elasticity with Endogenous Deductions

In general the elasticity of deductions with respect to gross profits, $\eta_{D,P}$, is non-zero and its behaviour has an important impact on revenue elasticities, as seen from equation (2.6). Deductions available to be claimed depend, for example, on investment, via capital allowances, and on past profits and losses of the company. In the case of a company within a group, deductions also depend on group members' profits and losses. This subsection considers the effects of these on the revenue elasticity.

To the extent that deductions are mainly composed of capital allowances, and investment expenditure rises with profits, this tends to increase deductions (with a lag), so that $dD/dP > 0$. On the other hand, losses would be expected to fall as profits rise, so that $dD/dP < 0$ is more likely. Defining capital allowances and losses claimed against profits, as CA and LC respectively, consider two extreme cases. First, a given level of D is made up entirely of capital allowances, so that $D = CA$, and second, the same level of D is composed entirely of losses claimed, so that $D = LC$. For a given level of profits, the term $P/(P-D)$ in (2.6) is the same for both cases and is greater than 1.

If investment is positively correlated with profits, $dD/dP > 0$ for capital allowances, whereas $dD/dP < 0$ for losses. For illustration, let $dCA/dP = \varepsilon$ and $dLC/dP = -\varepsilon$. Thus the first term in brackets in (2.6) becomes $1-\varepsilon$ for capital allowances, but $1+\varepsilon$ for losses. That is, losses contribute to the revenue elasticity exceeding 1 (recalling that $\frac{P}{P-D} > 1$), whereas capital allowances encourage a revenue elasticity less than 1. It becomes less than 1 if $1 - \varepsilon$ outweighs $\frac{P}{P-D}$ in (2.6). Of course, both deductions also have 'level' effects which raise the elasticity, since greater deduction levels imply larger values of $\frac{P}{P-D}$.

2.2.1 Group Relief

It is readily shown that the availability of group relief (compared with no group relief deductions or single firms only) leads to higher revenue elasticities for companies which remain taxpayers, and zero elasticities for previous taxpayers whose liabilities are reduced to zero. Consider, for example, the case of two firms, i and j, where i is in profit while j makes a loss. In the absence of group relief, or for single companies, the elasticity of firm j is zero, while j's elasticity exceeds unity depending on the value of net profits, $P_i - D_i$.

Suppose group relief becomes available, or the two companies form a group. Firm j is able to transfer some or all of it's losses to its partner. In this case j's elasticity remains zero, but deductions for the profit-maker have increased by the value of transferred losses. Firm i's elasticity therefore increases – the denominator in the elasticity falls. In terms of Figure 2.1, the profit-maker's schedule WXX'Y shifts rightwards by the amount of transferred losses, $D_2 - D_1$; this is shown in Figure 2.2.

At each gross profit, in excess of the new deductions level, D_2, for firm i, the revenue elasticity is greater than previously. However, for companies which are removed from taxpaying status as a result of group relief, those between D_1 and D_2, the revenue elasticity falls to zero. The effect of group relief on the revenue elasticity therefore depends on the relative sizes of the positive profits and group-relieved losses within the group. However, in a subsequent period, if the previously loss-making

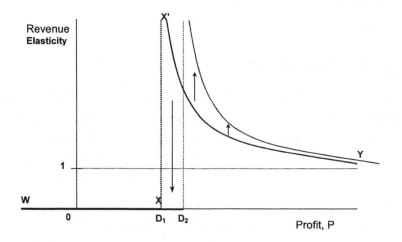

Figure 2.2: Elasticity with Varying Deductions

firm were to become a taxpayer, it would not have access to its previous losses as a profit offset. Hence its revenue elasticity would be lower than it would be without the use of group relief: in terms of Figure 2.2 it would be further to the right.

This result also demonstrates the impact on the elasticity of companies amalgamating to form groups. Amalgamation will cause the revenue elasticity to increase for those profit-making group members which remain taxpayers, compared with their previous single status. However, for previous profit-making companies whose profits are now eliminated by transferred losses, the elasticity falls to zero. The elasticities of previous loss-making companies are unaffected by amalgamation – they remain zero. Again, however, their future elasticities are also affected by the surrender of their current losses.

2.2.2 Consolidated Accounting

A move to consolidated accounting whereby group, rather than company, profits form the tax base, would have a similar effect to group relief. However, consolidation would effectively allow some losses, which remain 'stranded' under the current UK group relief system, to be deducted from group profits. In terms of Figure 2.2 this implies a greater rightward shift of the elasticity profile compared with the group relief case. Thus a greater range of positive profits would yield a zero revenue elasticity, but the elasticities associated with the higher tax-liable profit levels would increase. This should not be confused with the fact that, for given profit levels, tax levels are lower with consolidation. Rather, the higher revenue elasticity for taxpaying groups, with consolidation, implies that revenues grow faster relative to profits, than previously. Hence, faster tax growth is gained at the cost of lower initial tax levels, unless other tax parameters are changed.

2.2.3 Cyclical Effects

Figures 2.1 and 2.2 are less useful to illustrate the impact on revenue elasticities of economic booms and recessions, when deductions are expected to respond to cyclical changes in profits. An economic downturn is typically associated both with declining profits in taxpaying firms and greater losses among loss-makers. Where losses dominate deductions, $dD/dP < 0$ is more likely, and equation (2.6) showed the impact on the firm's revenue elasticity if it remains a taxpayer. Of course, cyclical fluctuations can also be expected to shift some firms into and out of taxpaying status. Clearly, how gross profits and deduction change over the economic cycle is crucial for the value of the revenue elasticity both of individual firms, and of firms in aggregate. This is explored further in Section 2.4. First, the next section considers the determinants of the corporation tax revenue elasticity aggregated across all firms, and the role of the corporation tax schedule.

2.3   The Tax Schedule and Revenue Elasticities

For an individual firm, the tax revenue elasticity, $\eta_{T,P}$, in equation (2.6) has been defined above as:

$$\eta_{T,P} = \frac{dT}{dP}\frac{P}{T} = \frac{MTR}{ATR} \tag{2.8}$$

where MTR and ATR are the marginal and average tax rates (defined with respect to *gross* profit) facing the firm, and referred to below as the *Gross MTR* and *ATR*. Since the UK corporation tax 'schedule' describes the relationship between tax liabilities and net, rather than gross, profits, it is useful to decompose this elasticity into two components. Hence:

$$\eta_{T,P} = \left(\eta_{T,P^T}\right)\left(\eta_{P^T,P}\right) \tag{2.9}$$

Equation (2.9) expresses $\eta_{T,P}$ as the product of the elasticity of tax paid with respect to net profits, η_{T,P^T}, and the elasticity of net profits to gross profits, $\eta_{P^T,P}$. The first component elasticity is determined by the corporation tax 'schedule'. In the UK this involves four net profit thresholds, $m_0, ..., m_4$, two tax rates t_1 and t_2, and two 'marginal relief fractions', F_1 and F_2. A firm's tax liability within each range is given in Table 2.1.

Table 2.1: The Corporate Tax Schedule

Profit Range	Tax
$P^T m_0$	$T\left(P^T\right) = 0$
$m_0 < P^T m_1$	$T\left(P^T\right) = t_1 P^T - F_1\left(m_1 - P^T\right)$
$m_1 < P^T m_2$	$T\left(P^T\right) = t_1 P^T$
$m_2 < P^T m_3$	$T\left(P^T\right) = t_2 P^T - F_2\left(m_3 - P^T\right)$
$P^T > m_3$	$T\left(P^T\right) = t_2 P^T$

It can be seen that there are two ranges of net profit, $m_1 < P^T m_2$ and $P^T > m_3$ where taxation is a fixed proportion of net profit, t_1 and t_2 respectively, otherwise this proportion varies. Since the corporation tax schedule specifies the relationship between the corporation tax paid, T, and *net* profit, P^T, *Net* average and marginal tax rates may be defined as:

$$ATR(P^T) = \frac{T(P^T)}{P^T} \tag{2.10}$$

and:

$$MTR(P^T) = \frac{dT}{dP^T} \tag{2.11}$$

and the revenue elasticity component in (2.9), η_{T,P^T}, is simply:

$$\eta_{T,P^T} = \left\{ \frac{MTR(P^T)}{ATR(P^T)} \right\}$$

The *Net ATRs* and *MTRs* associated with each net profit range in Table 2.1, are shown in Table 2.2, and illustrated in Figure 2.3. These are based on current UK parameter values; see Table 2.3. For example, over the range $m_0 P^T m_1$ the $ATR(P^T)$ gradually increases from 0 to t_1, such that:

$$ATR(P^T) = \frac{T\left(P^T\right)}{P^T} = t_1 - F_1\left(\frac{m_1}{P^T} - 1\right) \tag{2.12}$$

and t_1 is reduced by a fraction of the proportional difference between m_1 and net profit. The parameter values apply to single firms where no group relief is relevant. In the case of company groups, the profit thresholds, m_0 to m_4, are divided by the number of firms in the group, and the marginal relief fractions adjusted accordingly.

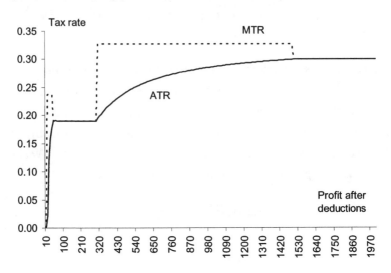

Figure 2.3: Marginal and Average Tax Rates

The tax schedule obviously differs from a typical income tax schedule where, for example, a higher tax rate is applied only to income measured above the relevant threshold, and lower ranges of income are taxed at lower rates. For a firm with P^T in excess of m_3, *all* of net taxable profit is subject to the higher rate of t_2. The two marginal relief fractions are determined in order to ensure that there are no discontinuities in the tax schedule. For example, $T\left(P^T = m_0\right) = 0 = t_1 m_0 - F_1\left(m_1 - m_0\right)$, so that $F_1 = t_1 m_0 / \left(m_1 - m_0\right)$. Similarly, $T\left(P^T = m_2\right) = t_1 m_2 = t_2 m_2 - F_2\left(m_3 - m_2\right)$, and thus $F_2 = \{m_2\left(t_2 - t_1\right)\} / \left(m_3 - m_2\right)$.

These properties mean that although $T\left(P^T\right) / P^T$ is either

Table 2.2: Net Average and Marginal Tax Rates

Profit Range	$ATR(P^T)$	$MTR(P^T)$
$P^T m_0$	0	0
$m_0 < P^T m_1$	$t_1 - F_1 \left(\frac{m_1}{P^T} - 1 \right)$	$t_1 + F_1$
$m_1 < P^T m_2$	t_1	t_1
$m_2 < P^T m_3$	$t_2 - F_2 \left(\frac{m_2}{P^T} - 1 \right)$	$t_2 + F_2$
$P^T > m_3$	t_2	t_2

constant or increasing, the tax schedule as a whole does not display marginal tax rate progression. As Figure 2.3 shows, over the range $m_0 < P^T m_1$ the term $dT/dP^T = t_1 + F_1$, and this falls to t_1 over the range $m_1 < P^T m_2$. Similarly, dT/dP^T falls from $t_2 + F_2$ over the range $m_2 < P^T m_3$, to t_2 when $P^T > m_3$.

Table 2.3: Parameters of the CT Schedule: 2006

Parameter	Value	Parameter	Value
m_0	$10k$	t_1	0.19
m_1	$50k$	t_2	0.30
m_2	$300k$	F_1	$19/400$
m_3	$1500k$	F_2	$11/400$

The resulting elasticity of tax with respect to net profits, η_{T,P^T}, is illustrated in Figure 2.4. It can be seen that this elasticity is constant (and equals 1) above m_3, and for $m_1 < P^T m_2$, but otherwise it varies with P^T. This component, η_{T,P^T}, of the overall revenue elasticity, $\eta_{T,P}$, is potentially important for understanding the revenue responsiveness of small firms since, as Figure 2.4 illustrates, this can vary substantially with net profit levels below m_3.

However, total corporation tax revenues are dominated by revenues from large firms, where $P^T > m_3$. For those firms, $\eta_{T,P^T} = 1$ and the elasticity of net profit with respect to gross profit is the sole determinant of the total revenue elasticity, $\eta_{T,P}$.

That is, for $P^T > m_3$:

$$\eta_{T,P} = \eta_{P^T,P} \qquad (2.13)$$

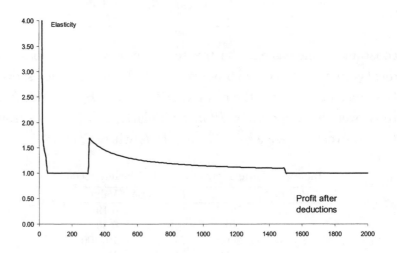

Figure 2.4: Revenue Elasticity of Tax with Respect to Net Profits

Thus, for most large firms the elasticity properties of the corporate tax are complicated not so much by the nature of the tax schedule as by the complexities involved in the transformation from P to P^T. As shown in equation (2.6) above, this elasticity is far from straightforward, and depends on the level of, and changes in, deductions relative to net or gross profits. The ratio of deductions to profits is not in general constant but is likely to vary over the economic cycle. As a result, the tax revenue elasticity can also be expected to vary systematically over the cycle. This is the subject of the following section.

2.4 The Aggregate Revenue Elasticity

For governments interested in raising revenues, the major policy concern is typically with the behaviour of aggregate, rather than individual firms', tax revenue. A corresponding aggregate revenue elasticity can be defined as follows. Let $P = \sum_{i=1}^{n} P_i$ and $T = \sum_{i=1}^{n} T_i$ denote aggregate profits and aggregate revenue, where there are $i = 1, ..., n$ firms. The change in total tax revenue is therefore:

$$dT = \sum_{i=1}^{n} \frac{dT_i}{dP_i} dP_i \qquad (2.14)$$

Defining the aggregate revenue elasticity as $\eta = \frac{dT}{dP}\frac{P}{T}$, it can be shown from (2.14) that the aggregate revenue elasticity is:

$$\eta = \sum_{i=1}^{n} \left(\eta_{T_i, P_i}\right) \left(\eta_{P_i, P}\right) \left(\frac{T_i}{T}\right) \qquad (2.15)$$

where η_{T_i, P_i} is the elasticity for an individual firm, T_i/T is the share of firm i's tax payments in total tax revenue, and $\eta_{P_i, P}$ is the elasticity of the each firm's profits with respect to total profits. This last elasticity depends on changes in the distribution of profits. It would be equal to 1 if all profits were to change in equal proportions. However, this is not typically the case, with profit growth rates often quite different across firms; indeed it is common for some firms to move into loss whilst others move in the opposite direction. As a result, profit dynamics can be expected to be important for estimates of aggregate revenue elasticities, and the aggregate revenue elasticity is not amenable to tractable analytical solutions.

2.4.1   The Revenue Elasticity over the Cycle

This subsection considers the likely pattern of the aggregate revenue elasticity when profits cycle round a trend growth rate. Deductions against corporation tax in the UK are dominated by losses and capital allowances claimed, and these can be expected to display both trend and cyclical aspects. For example, in 2004 losses used and capital allowances accounted for over 85 per cent of all deductions claimed against corporation tax in the UK. The aggregate elasticity, as given in equation (2.15), is a tax-share weighted average of the product of each firms' revenue elasticity and the elasticity of its profits with respect to aggregate profits. If all firms move together, so that there are no changes in relative profits among firms, the aggregate elasticity is $\eta = \sum_{i=1}^{n} \left(\eta_{T_i,P_i} \right) (T_i/T)$. In the trivial case where, for every firm, profits and deductions grow at the same rate, $dP_i/P_i = dD_i/D_i$ and the individual and aggregate revenue elasticities are all unity.

The key issue therefore is whether a steady long-run trend rate of profit growth is likely to produce the conditions under which the revenue elasticity is unity. During trend growth – though not within a cycle – it seems plausible that profits and deductions grow at similar rates. For firms which consistently make positive profits, and which therefore have no loss pools, deductions are composed of capital allowances, and it is not unreasonable to suppose that investment and profits grow at similar rates. For some firms the long-run trend growth of profits may at some point involve net profits turning from negative to positive, but the share of such firms' tax in total tax revenue is likely to be so small that they have little effect on the aggregate. Hence, over the long run a corporate tax revenue elasticity approximately equal to one can be expected, at least in the UK where losses and capital allowances dominate deductions claimed against corporation tax.

However, within an economic cycle these conditions cannot be expected to hold, as company losses and investment vary from year to year in response to economic conditions. In those periods of the cycle which have rising profits, the growth of tax revenue is likely to be lower than that of profits since loss pools – accumulated during the previous low point of the cycle – can be deducted against profits. Conversely, when profits are in the falling stages of the cycle, those loss pools will typically have been exhausted in the previous high point, so taxation is not expected to fall as fast as profits. Hence, it is likely that aggregate tax revenue follows a smoother cycle than that of profits. A key source of this smoothing effect is that, whereas companies' gross profits (as measured in company accounts, for example) can become negative, the net taxable profits on which corporation tax liability is assessed cannot be negative.[1]

This cyclical pattern is shown in Figure 2.5 using a sine wave to depict the economic cycle for both (gross) profits and taxes, and in which profit and tax growth is always positive. As Figure 2.5 shows, profit growth above trend implies elasticity values less than 1, whilst profit growth below trend implies elasticities greater than 1. That is, the corporation tax revenue elasticity would appear to be counter-cyclical.

A similar cycle is depicted in Figure 2.6 but in this case profit

---

[1]Data on the HMRC measure of gross profits would not necessarily display this property since negative gross profits (gross losses) are recorded for tax purposes as zero gross profits. Losses appear instead as an offset claimed against positive gross profits.

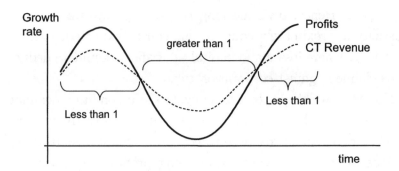

Figure 2.5: Moderate Cycle

growth becomes negative at the bottom of the cycle, whereas tax growth remains positive. This has a dramatic effect on the cyclical aspect of the revenue elasticity, which now exceeds 1 when profit growth is below trend but still positive, and the elasticity becomes negative at the bottom of the cycle when profit growth is negative. Finally, Figure 2.7 shows that if the cyclical downturn is sufficiently severe such that both tax and profit growth become negative, this generates even more volatility in the revenue elasticity.

Illustrative revenue elasticity profiles for the types of cycle depicted in Figures 2.6 and 2.7 are shown in Figures 2.8 and 2.9. These are constructed using a cycle based on a sine wave with values as shown in Table 2.4. The values shown are within the range of observed profit growth rates given in Chapter 1 in Figure 1.3, and were obtained from sine waves with an amplitude of 20 (profits) and 7 (tax) around trend growth shown in the table. A wavelength of 15 was used.

It is clear from these illustrative diagrams that the revenue elasticity can be highly volatile over the cycle, especially during

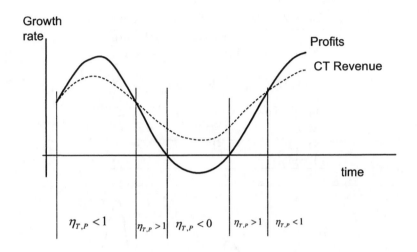

Figure 2.6: A Cycle with Negative Profit Growth

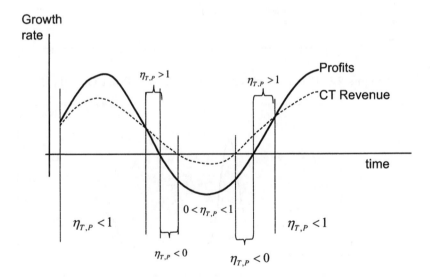

Figure 2.7: A Cycle with Negative Profit and Tax Growth

Table 2.4: Profit and Tax Growth Rates

| | Percentage growth rates ||
	Profits	Taxation
Figure 2.8		
Max	30	17
Min	-10	3
Trend	10	10
Figure 2.9		
Max	25	12
Trend	-15	-2
Trend	5	5

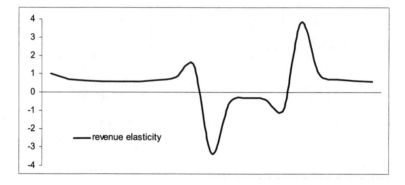

Figure 2.8: Elasticity with Negative Minimum Profit Growth

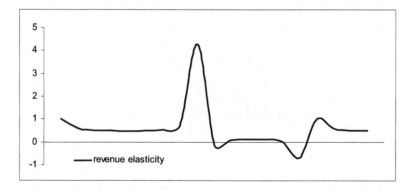

Figure 2.9: Elasticity with Negative Minimum Profit and Tax Growth

economic downturns. In the case where only profit growth becomes negative in a downturn, the revenue elasticity can take large negative values, as well as relatively large positive values either side of the downturn. When tax growth can also become negative, it can be seen in Figure 2.9 that negative revenue elasticities are smaller and much less persistent but large positive elasticities are possible going into a downturn. These highly volatile revenue elasticities are of course obtained using a regular smooth cycle for profits and taxes, suggesting that with more erratic profit growth rates, revenue elasticities are likely to be even more volatile.

2.5 Conclusions

This chapter has concentrated on the central concept of the corporation tax revenue elasticity, for individual firms and in aggregate. Deductions, and how they change as profits grow, were seen to play a crucial role in determining whether corporation tax revenues are expected to grow faster or slower than profits. Additionally for small firms, the nature of the corporate tax schedule – the tax rates and thresholds applied to net profits – can be important for their revenue elasticities.

The analysis highlighted the role of cyclical factors. It is important to determine when, and to what extent, the corporation tax revenue elasticity deviates from its expected long-run value of 1, when tax and profits grow at the same rate. First, the volatility observed in corporation tax buoyancy is also found to characterise the corporation tax revenue elasticity. This implies that much of the observed volatility in corporation tax receipts and accruals could indeed be inherent to the corporation tax system, given the volatility in the tax base, profits.

In mild economic downturns, corporation tax revenue elasticities may rise (because tax growth falls less than profit growth), but in more severe downturns, large but temporary increases and decreases in the revenue elasticity (and even negative elasticities) can be expected. Over the long run (of one or more full economic cycles), corporation tax revenues and profits can be expected to grow at around the same rate (in the absence of discretionary changes in tax rates, compliance and so on). Nevertheless, annual averages of revenue elasticities are a misleading guide to long-run tax growth. The analysis suggests that forecasting corporation tax revenues is likely to be especially difficult during pronounced economic downturns, but can be expected to be less problematic for above-trend fluctuations when corporate losses are less prevalent. Part IV below considers this issue further, using simulations based on the model developed in Part III.

Chapter 3

Tax Loss Asymmetries

The corporation tax treatment of losses typically involves an asymmetry in the tax function in that losses do not give rise to a tax rebate equivalent to the tax on positive profits. Often losses can only be used concurrently if they can offset positive profits from other sources within the corporation, or across members of a group of 'associated' corporations defined for tax purposes. Donnelly and Young (2002, pp. 446-449) reviewed the tax treatment of groups of companies in 30 OECD countries, of which two thirds allow some form of group relief. Alternatively they can be carried forward or back to be used as profit offsets in future or previous periods. There are sometimes restrictions on flexibility when losses are used in this way. For example, in the UK schedular system some loss pools can be used only as offsets against the same source, whereas current losses can be used contemporaneously against profits from different sources. For multinational corporations, losses in overseas subsidiaries cannot be offset against profits arising in the UK.

The overall effect of these restrictions is that some losses become 'stranded', even if temporarily, such that the effective 'rate of rebate' on losses is less than the rate of tax on profits. These sources of asymmetry apply, for example, to the UK and US corporation tax regimes, leading Cooper and Knittel (2006, p. 651) to conclude for the US that, 'many tax losses are used with a substantial delay' so that 'certain firms and industries suffer a significant penalty from the partial loss refund regime due to the erosion in the real value of their loss refund'. They also report (2006, p. 651) that up to 50 per cent of corporate losses remain unused after ten years, and that around 25–30 per cent of losses are never used.[1] For the UK, Klemm and McCrae (2002) reported that Inland Revenue estimates suggest that in the UK a higher proportion of about 80 per cent of losses arising in 2000–01 were used as tax offsets in that same year: see Devereux (1989) for earlier evidence on the extent of losses in the UK. This asymmetry aquires particular importance in view of the large size of losses, amounting to about £80bn in the UK in 2000-01 and $418bn in the US in 2002.

The effect on investment behaviour of this asymmetry has been investigated by Auerbach (1986), Devereux (1989), Altshuler and Auerbach (1990) and Edgerton (2007). The importance of asymmetry for companies' average tax rates was stressed by Auerbach (2007), who showed that, *ceteris paribus*, restrictions on loss use have significantly increased US corporations' implicit average tax rates above statutory rates, especially during cyclical downturns. He also argued that, although

---

[1]See also Office of Tax Policy (2007), which also compares policies in G-7 countries, and suggests that the asymmetry reduces the automatic stabilization properties of taxes and encourages uneconomic mergers, as well as affecting investment incentives. For some deductions against profits, such as allowances for investment expenditures, the effective rebate rate can exceed the rate of tax on profits if, for example, the capital allowance regime is designed to be especially generous, perhaps to encourage investment. The present chapter is concerned only with loss asymmetries and hence ignores this possibility but the analysis below carries over in a straightforward fashion to the case where the asymmetry involves a more, rather than less, generous tax deduction.

US corporations have generally been making greater losses since the early 1980s, they have been using them less to offset their corporate tax liabilities, so raising their effective average tax rates. This led Auerbach to cast doubt on arguments that US corporates are increasingly avoiding tax by engaging in international profit-shifting.

This chapter provides an analysis of how the asymmetric treatment of losses can be expected to affect companies' behavioural responses to changes in tax rates, as measured by the elasticity of tax revenue with respect to the tax rate. It introduces the concept of an equivalent tax function, raising the same present value of tax payments as the actual function, but in which the effective rate on losses in any period, and thus the degree of asymmetry, is explicit. The influence of this effective rate on the variation in the elasticity of tax revenue with respect to the corporate tax rate over the business cycle is then examined. Cooper and Knittel (2006, p. 663) concluded that future work 'should examine how the time delay in loss utilization manifests itself in marginal tax rate discrepancies between industries and over time'.

This tax revenue elasticity has been the focus of a number of empirical studies of corporate profit-shifting, such as Demirgüç-Kunt and Huizinga (2001), Bartelsman and Beetsma (2003) and Huizinga and Laeven (2007). In some case these authors report semi-elasticities of tax revenue, or taxable profits, with respect to the tax rate. For recent evidence relating to Europe, see Dischinger (2007). Responses to corporation tax changes can take two forms. First, there are real responses, whereby activities are transferred to other tax jurisdictions. The second form of response involves income-shifting in which the location of economic activity is unchanged but the extent to which profits and deductions are declared in the home country changes, for example through the use of transfer pricing. The present chapter does not separate these responses but shows that overall behavioural responses of tax revenue to tax rate changes depend crucially on the extent of the tax function asymmetry. Since losses can be expected to vary over the economic cycle, it is shown that the asymmetric treatment of losses generates effects on tax revenue elasticities that are asymmetric between above-trend and below-trend parts of the cycle.

Section 3.1 considers the tax treatment of losses in the context of a single corporation and provides a precise measure of the asymmetry involved. While concentration on a single firm is somewhat artificial in this context, it avoids the unnecessary complications arising from modelling a distribution of firms' profits and losses, and focuses on the key asymmetry that applies to individual corporations. Section 3.2 demonstrates the role of this tax asymmetry in the analysis of the behavioural responsiveness of revenue to tax rate changes. Section 3.3 illustrates the magnitude of the elasticity of tax revenue with respect to the tax rate during periods of above-trend and below-trend growth, comparing symmetric and asymmetric loss treatments. It is shown that the asymmetric treatment of losses reduces size of the behavioural component of the tax revenue elasticity compared with their symmetric treatment. It also gives rise to asymmetric behaviour of the elasticity over the business cycle which becomes more pronounced as company profits (net of losses) move further below trend, but not when they move further above trend.

3.1 Taxes and Loss Asymmetries

This section provides a framework for examining the value of losses as profit offsets in the context of a single corporation with more than one profit source. Subsection 3.1.1 considers the relationship between losses and deductions, and subsection 3.1.2 provides some numerical illustrations. The approach involves defining the value of losses as tax deductions in present value terms under the alternatives of symmetric and asymmetric treatment. This allows an effective tax rate on losses to be derived.

3.1.1 Losses and Deductions

Consider a firm obtaining profits from several sources. Some of these generate positive profits in time period j with a total of P_j. Other sources produce total losses during j of L_j. To focus on the asymmetric treatment of losses, assume that losses are the only deductions allowable against profits in determining corporate tax liabilities. The typical tax function can be described as having a constant marginal tax rate, t, applied to taxable profits. As discussed in Chapter 2, in the UK there is a lower rate band and other bands where the marginal rate varies, but the vast majority of tax is paid at the single higher rate. The *actual* tax liability that a corporation faces in period j, T_j^A, is given by the function:

$$T_j^A = t\left(P_j - D_j\right) \tag{3.1}$$

where D_j is the value of loss deductions offset in period j, such that:

$$D_j = \min(P_j, L_j + L_j^P) \tag{3.2}$$

where L_j^P represents the 'loss pool' carried over from the previous period, consisting of unused earlier losses. In practice some companies may not claim all the tax loss deductions to which they are entitled: this complication is ignored here. Any losses in excess of P_j are then carried forwards (or backwards) to be offset in future (or previous) periods, depending on the time profile of past and future profits and losses.

The restriction in (3.2) produces the fundamental corporation tax asymmetry. Whereas the tax liability for each additional unit of profit generated in period j is t, the negative tax liability on each extra unit of losses generated in j is not $-t$. Rather, it depends on the future or past periods, if any, for which tax code restrictions allow these losses to be used as tax offsets. For this reason it is important to compare the tax liabilities associated with profits and losses generated in a given period in present value terms. For example, if limited future profits mean that some period j losses are never used as offsets for tax purposes then the tax (or rebate) rate on those losses is effectively zero. On the other hand, if all period j losses can be used to reduce future, but not current, tax liabilities, they have a tax liability in present value terms that is greater than $-t$ (that is, an effective rebate rate of less than t). The precise magnitude depends on the relevant time profile of loss offsets and the associated discount rate. The relevant tax rate on losses therefore lies between $-t$ and 0.

The effective tax rate applied to losses at any time is therefore not transparent from (3.1), as the present value of losses as tax offsets does not appear in the tax function. However, it is the effective rate that is required in order to examine the incentives facing firms regarding their real and profit-shifting responses to tax changes. Any current loss involves a time stream of tax offsets which needs to be captured in some way. The following analysis produces an appropriate framework. First, it is convenient to ignore the 'carry back' of losses, as this does not affect the argument. Also uncertainty regarding future profits and losses is ignored: the fundamental issue concerns the nature of the time profiles rather than uncertainty.

The objective is to construct an alternative tax function which collects the same present value of tax revenue from the firm as the actual tax function, over the period during which the losses are able to be used as offsets. This time period is not necessarily fixed, though a time limit may be specified in the tax code. Donnelly and Young (2002, p. 448) summarise the time restrictions, along with provisions for group allowances, in OECD countries. The 'parameters' of the function, expressed in terms of a single-period tax schedule, need to encapsulate the use of the losses in such a way that allows subsequent analysis to trace how the effective tax rate varies for different assumptions about the time profile of profits and the nature of the asymmetric treatment of losses.

Define q_j as the proportion of losses arising in period j which are used as a deduction in period j. Furthermore, define q_{j+k}, as the proportion of the j losses used as tax offsets in period $j + k$. These proportions are determined by the firm's profits and losses in period j and future profits and losses over periods $k = 1, 2, \ldots$ and so on. For example, if the firm expects a profit in $j+k$ of P_{j+k}, and it expects to be able to use some of j's losses (depending on their earlier use) to offset part of those profits, say an amount equal to $P_{j+k}^* < P_{j+k}$, then $q_{j+k} = P_{j+k}^*/L_j$. It is appropriate here to assume that earlier losses, if any exist, are used before current losses. In practice, as mentioned above, loss pools may be less flexible than current lossses.

Let s_j denote the present value at j, of period j's losses as tax offsets, as a proportion of their nominal value L_j, over the relevant period. Letting r denote the discount rate, s_j is given by:

$$s_j = q_j + \frac{q_{j+1}}{1+r} + \frac{q_{j+2}}{(1+r)^2} + \dots \tag{3.3}$$

where summation is over the relevant time horizon, say K. As mentioned earlier, the time horizon itself depends both on the tax code and the firm's time profile of profits and losses. See Devereux (1989, p.105) for a comparable expression for the effective tax rate associated with capital allowances. Thus:

$$s_j = \sum_{k=0}^{K} \frac{q_{j+k}}{(1+r)^k} \tag{3.4}$$

where $0 < s_j < 1$. The first term q_j ($k = 0$), is simply, as defined above, the proportion of losses arising in j that are used in period j. Each subsequent term, for periods $j + k$, where $k = 1, ..., K$, reflects the suitably discounted proportions of period j losses which are used in periods $j + k$.

The corporation's tax liability in period j, T_j, can therefore be defined using an alternative function given by:

$$T_j = t\left(P_j - s_j L_j\right) \tag{3.5}$$

where t is the proportional tax rate as defined in the actual tax function, and there is no restriction preventing a rebate in j if $s_j L_j > P_j$. It can be shown that the present value of tax payments is the same under (3.5) as with the actual tax function.

The term s_j may be referred to as the loss 'deductions rate'. By defining the deductions value of losses in this way, the average and marginal 'rates of deduction', s, are assumed to be the same. This could be relaxed (for example, by defining $D = s_0 + sL$, where D is the deductions value of losses) but the simpler form here is sufficient to demonstrate the impact of the asymmetries of interest. For simplicity, expected future tax rates are assumed constant here; Appendix A shows how s_j can be redefined if t is exected to vary.

The company's effective tax rate on losses in j is therefore $-s_j t$. In the case of symmetric tax treatment of profits and losses, $s_j = 1$. The asymmetry is demonstrated in Figure 3.1 where the tax function in (3.5), T_j, is the solid line. The symmetric case is represented by a linear function, such that tax and rebate schedules are mirror images. The actual tax function in (3.1) follows the horizontal axis until $P_j > D_j$, after which it slopes upwards at the rate, t.

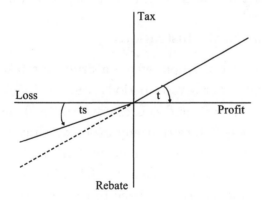

Figure 3.1: The Asymmetric Treatment of Losses

The value of s_j can be related to Auerbach's (2007) comparison of the statutory tax rate, t, and implicit average tax rate, τ, faced by companies. Define the implicit average tax rate in period j as $\tau_j = T_j/(P_j - L_j)$. It is then readily shown from (3.5) that:

$$\frac{\tau_j}{t} = \frac{P_j - s_j L_j}{P_j - L_j} \tag{3.6}$$

Furthermore, defining the ratio of net profit to positive profit as $\theta_j = (P_j - L_j)/P_j$, for $P_j > 0$, this becomes:

$$\frac{\tau_j}{t} = \frac{1 - s_j(1 - \theta_j)}{\theta_j} \tag{3.7}$$

When the function is symmetric $s_j = 1$ and $\tau_j = t$. The result in (3.7) demonstrates the combined impact on the ratio of τ_j to t of s_j and the economic cycle, since $1 - \theta_j$ captures the ratio of company losses to profits. In particular, τ_j/t is expected to rise during cyclical downturns, as observed by Auerbach (2007) for the US. An additional effect arising when there is a positive correlation between s_j and θ_j, is discussed in section 3.2.

3.1.2 Numerical Illustrations

Consider a simple example where a firm undertakes only one type of activity over several periods. Hence if $P_j > 0$ it must be true that $L_j = 0$, and conversely if $L_j > 0$ then $P_j = 0$. Let the tax code dictate that any losses which cannot be used immediately can only be carried forward and used against future profits within the firm. This and the following example assume that losses cannot be carried back to earlier periods, or across firms.

Assume further that if losses are not used as tax off-sets within three years, they will not be usable at all, so that $K = 3$.

This helps to illustrate stranded losses. The firm's actual profit in period j and its expected profits and losses, for $k = 1, ..., 3$, are shown in Table 3.1. There is a loss in only period j and positive profits in $j + k$, so in this example concern is simply with the value of s_j (all $s_{j+k} = 0$).

Table 3.1: Example 1

Period	j	$j+1$	$j+2$	$j+3$
Profits/losses	-500	100	100	100
Losses used	0	100	100	100
Losses available	500	400	300	200

The example shows that a loss of \$500 in period j is used to offset profits of \$100 in each of three subsequent years. Given the time limitation, 200 of period j's losses are 'stranded'. Hence $q_j = 0$ and $q_{j+k} = 100/500 = 1/5$ for $k = 1, ..., 3$. Using a discount rate of 10 per cent, s_j is calculated, by substituting in (3.3), as:

$$
\begin{aligned}
s_j &= 0 + \left(\frac{1}{5(1.1)}\right) + \left(\frac{1}{5(1.1)^2}\right) + \left(\frac{1}{5(1.1)^3}\right) \\
&= 0 + 0.182 + 0.165 + 0.150 \\
&= 0.497
\end{aligned}
\tag{3.8}
$$

Here $s_j < 1$ because of the fact that, by assumption, losses in period j cannot be used beyond $j + 3$ and because their use in future profit-making periods must be discounted to produce the present value. It can be seen that the present value of tax liabilities for the four years under the equivalent function in (3.5), T_j, is:

$$
\begin{aligned}
T_j &= t\left\{-500(0.497) + 100/1.1 + 100/1.1^2 + 100/1.1^3\right\} \\
&= 0
\end{aligned}
\tag{3.9}
$$

which is the same as the actual tax payments, T_j^A, of zero under
an asymmetric structure, allowing losses to be carried forward
for only three periods.

Consider a second example, in which there are two profit
schedules, A and B. Source A makes positive profits in each
period while source B makes losses in each period. These B
losses are allowed to be carried forward and offset against A
profits. The firm is assumed to use the earliest available vintage
of losses first. Rows 2 and 3 of Table 3.2 show the stream of A
profits and B losses over 5 periods. Row 4 shows the losses used
within each period, with those brought forward from previous
periods. Losses carried forward to the next period are shown in
row 5. The time profiles of profits and losses are such that there
are no losses in period 5; hence $s_5 = 0$.

Table 3.2: Example 2

1	Period (j)	1	2	3	4	5
2	A profits	20	20	10	10	10
3	B losses	25	20	15	10	0
4	B losses used	20	$5 + 15$	$5 + 5$	**10**	**10**
5	B losses c/f	5	5	10	10	0
6	s_j		0.982	0.977	0.939	0.909	0

Unlike the earlier simple case, this example shows values of
s_j for $j = 1, ..., 5$. In each case, the profiles of profits and losses
are such that losses in j are exhausted in $j + 1$, so only two
terms are needed in obtaining the sum in equation (3.4), and no
losses are stranded. In each of the periods 1 to 4 some losses
are carried forward to be used in the next period, so they are
discounted at $r = 0.1$. The values carried forward are shown
in bold. Consider the case of $j = 1$, where $q_j = 20/25$ and

$q_{j+1} = 5/25$. Substitution in (3.3) gives:

$$s_1 = \frac{20}{25} + \left(\frac{5}{25}\right)\left(\frac{1}{1.1}\right) = 0.982 \qquad (3.10)$$

The values of s_j for subsequent periods are shown in the last row of the table. It can be seen that s_j falls from period 1 and is zero in period 5 when losses are zero. The declining value of s_j reflects the fact that in each successive period an increasing fraction of each period's losses are carried forward before they are used as deductions: these are: 5/25; 5/20; 10/15; and 10/10. Hence a greater fraction of losses are subject to discounting. In this second example, based on the actual tax function, the firm pays no tax in each of the five periods. Again, this is the same as the present value of tax liabilities in the equivalent function (3.5) for the five periods, since:

$$
\begin{aligned}
\frac{T_j}{t} &= \{20 - 25\,(0.982)\} + \frac{\{20 - 20\,(0.977)\}}{1.1} \\
&+ \frac{\{10 - 15\,(0.939)\}}{1.1^2} + \frac{\{10 - 10\,(0.909)\}}{1.1^3} + \frac{10}{1.1^4} \\
&= 0
\end{aligned}
\qquad (3.11)
$$

As mentioned above, these examples exclude loss carry back. If this option were available the firm could effectively offset previous profits immediately (that is, in period j), such that if x is the value of previous profits available to be offset, q_j becomes x/L_j, subject to xL_j. There is no need to discount losses carried back since the tax code implies that period j losses are used concurrently, although in accounting terms they are offsetting previous profits.

Although the precise value of s_j has been seen to depend on the time profile of the firm's profits and losses, the specification

of the equivalent tax function using this concept of asymmetry
has the advantage that it allows valuable insights to be obtained
into the determinants, and possible pattern over the business
cycle, of the elasticity of revenue with respect to the tax rate,
without having to specify the full time-profile of profits.[2] This
is explored in the following sections.

3.2   Responses to Tax Changes

The question of interest here is how the asymmetry in tax loss
treatment described in the previous section, and summarised by
s_j, affects the behavioural response of tax revenue to changes
in the corporate tax rate. The analysis in this section considers
an individual firm, though this does not preclude the possibility
that the losses available to that firm as tax offsets are generated
by a partner firm, to the extent that the tax code permits such
loss-sharing. The basic elasticity describing the behavioural responses to a tax rate change is discussed first in subsection 3.2.1
and the effects of changes in net profits over the business cycle
are examined in subsection 3.2.2.

3.2.1   Profit-Shifting and the Tax Rate

Consider a taxpaying firm for whom $P_j > s_j L_j$. From equation
(3.5), defining $P_j^T = P_j - s_j L_j$ as taxable profit, so that $T_j = t P_j^T$,
the effect on T_j of a change in the tax rate, t, is (omitting time

---

[2]However, the distribution of effective rates across firms could be obtained using the
simulation model discussed in Part III below. Effective rates were obtained, using simulation methods, by Myers and Majd (1986).

subscripts for convenience):

$$\frac{dT}{dt} = P^T + t\frac{dP^T}{dt} \qquad (3.12)$$

where dP^T/dt measures the extent of the corporation's response to the tax rate change. This includes any induced 'real' changes in profit levels arising from a change in location and profit shifts into or out of the tax jurisdiction. Dividing both sides of (3.12) by P^T and using the fact that $\frac{dT}{P^T dt} = \frac{t dT}{T dt} = \eta_{T,t}$:

$$\eta_{T,t} = 1 + \eta_{P^T,t} \qquad (3.13)$$

This uses the general notation $\eta_{x,y}$ to denote the elasticity of x with respect to y. The term $\eta_{P^T,t} \leq 0$ is the elasticity of taxable profits with respect to the tax rate, capturing possible behavioural responses. This elasticity is closely related to the Feldstein (1995, 1999) elasticity of taxable income with respect to the net-of-tax, or retention, rate, $\eta_{P^T,1-t}$, such that:

$$\eta_{P^T,t} = -\left(\frac{t}{1-t}\right)\eta_{P^T,1-t} \qquad (3.14)$$

Taxable profit, P_j^T, changes if either gross profits, P_j, or losses, L_j, alter in response to tax rate changes. It is useful for present purposes to define net profits as $N_j = P_j - L_j$ and work with the ratio of net profits to gross profits, θ_j, defined above. This allows the effects of the economic cycle to be examined by specifying systematic changes in θ_j over time. For $P_j > 0$:

$$\theta_j = N_j/P_j \qquad (3.15)$$

Losses can therefore be written as $L_j = (1 - \theta_j)P_j$. Substituting for L_j in the equivalent tax function of equation (3.5) allows the tax liability to be rewritten as:

$$T_j = t \{1 - s_j(1 - \theta_j)\} P_j \qquad (3.16)$$

Clearly, $\theta_j \leq 1$, but if $L_j > P_j$, θ_j can be negative. When $\theta_j < 0$, it is nevertheless possible to have $s_j(1 - \theta_j) < 1$ if s_j is sufficiently low, so that a positive tax payment is required in the equivalent function in period j even if losses exceed positive profits in the corporation.

However, s_j is a function of current and expected future profits and losses, and hence $s_j = s_j(\theta_j)$, with $ds_j/d\theta_j > 0$.[3] That is, a higher θ_j, implying lower reported losses for a given level of profits, raises the prospect that a given \$ of loss is used, or used sooner, to offset profits. In addition, to the extent that there is a behavioural response of declared losses to the tax rate, $\theta_j = \theta_j(t)$, where it is expected that $d\theta_j/dt_j < 0$ if increased tax rates encourage lower declared profits, or higher declared losses.

3.2.2   Tax and Net Profit Changes

In order to focus on the asymmetric impact of losses, the following analysis treats profits as fixed, that is, independent of the tax rate. Equivalent results in which either losses or θ is held fixed, while profits vary, could also be examined. Thus, emphasis is on the response of losses to tax rate change. In general, and omitting j subscripts for convenience, totally differentiating $T = T(t, \theta, s)$ and remembering that $s = s(\theta)$, gives:

$$\frac{dT}{dt} = \frac{\partial T}{\partial t} + \frac{\partial T}{\partial \theta}\frac{d\theta}{dt} + \frac{\partial T}{\partial s}\frac{\partial s}{\partial \theta}\frac{d\theta}{dt} \qquad (3.17)$$

---

[3]Strictly, allowing for future profits and losses, $s_j = s_j(\theta_{j+k})$, $k = 0, ..., K$. To keep the analytics simple, the additional complications arising from the effects on s_j of future values of θ are ignored below.

Multiplying both sides by t/T, and using the fact that the partial elasticity, $\frac{t\partial T}{T\partial t}$, is equal to 1 for a proportional tax structure, allows the elasticity, $\eta_{T,t}$, to be written as:

$$\eta_{T,t} = 1 + \eta_{T,\theta}\eta_{\theta,t} \tag{3.18}$$

where $\eta_{T,\theta}$ is:

$$\eta_{T,\theta} = \eta'_{T,\theta} + \eta'_{T,s}\eta'_{s,\theta} \tag{3.19}$$

The elasticities on the right-hand-side of (3.19), indicated by a prime, are partial elasticities associated with the partial derivatives in (3.17). The elasticity $\eta_{\theta,t}$ captures behavioural responses to tax rate changes associated with changes in losses, with an expected sign of $\eta_{\theta,t} < 0$. Thus an increase in the tax rate is expected to encourage a decrease in θ, reflecting an increase in losses declared for tax. This can arise either because real losses rise or losses generated elsewhere are shifted into the tax jurisdiction.

Other sign expectations are: $\eta'_{T,\theta} > 0$; $\eta'_{s,\theta} > 0$; and $\eta'_{T,s} < 0$. That is, a greater ratio of net-to-gross profits, θ, raises tax revenues directly and also raises s, since there are fewer losses competing to be offset against each unit of profit. However, the greater deductability of losses arising from a larger value of s reduces tax revenue.

Equation (3.19) demonstrates that any behavioural effect, captured by $\eta_{\theta,t}$, is transmitted into an effect on the tax revenue elasticity, $\eta_{T,t}$, via $\eta_{T,\theta}$, which in turn is determined by the sizes of $\eta'_{T,\theta}$ and $\eta'_{T,s}\eta'_{s,\theta}$. Any asymmetric effect on $\eta_{T,t}$ of losses must therefore arise via the direct effect, $\eta'_{T,\theta}$, and the indirect effect, $\eta'_{T,s}\eta'_{s,\theta}$, on tax revenues from changes in θ.

Expressions for the two partial elasticities $\eta'_{T,\theta}$ and $\eta'_{T,s}$ in terms of s and θ can be obtained by differentiating (3.16), whereby:

$$\eta'_{T,\theta} = \frac{s\theta}{1 - s(1 - \theta)} \tag{3.20}$$

and:

$$\eta'_{T,s} = \frac{-s(1 - \theta)}{1 - s(1 - \theta)} \tag{3.21}$$

If $s = 1$, so that the tax function is symmetric, (3.20) shows that $\eta'_{T,\theta} = 1$ and, since it must also be true in this case that $\eta'_{s,\theta} = 0$, (3.18) gives the simple result that:

$$\eta_{T,t} = 1 + \eta_{\theta,t} \tag{3.22}$$

Furthermore, if $\theta = 1$, so that the firm makes no losses from any source, a change whereby some losses are made (a fall in θ) implies $\eta'_{T,\theta} = s$.

Substituting (3.20) and (3.21) into (3.18) gives:

$$\eta_{T,t} = 1 + \left[\frac{s\left\{\theta - (1 - \theta)\eta'_{s,\theta}\right\}}{1 - s(1 - \theta)} \right] \eta_{\theta,t} \tag{3.23}$$

By comparison with (3.13), the second term in (3.23) is also $\eta_{PT,t}$. The component elasticities in (3.20) and (3.21) capture the impact of any asymmetries. They are respectively positive and negative for $0 < \theta < 1$, but the signs of $\eta'_{T,\theta}$ and $\eta'_{T,s}$ can be reversed when $\theta < 0$ (when losses exceed profits) depending on the values of θ and s. Thus, the value of $\eta_{T,t}$ in (3.23) depends, *inter alia*, on the extent of tax loss asymmetries, s, the economic cycle as captured by the ratio of net-to-gross profits, θ, together with the impact on s of changes in θ, $\eta'_{s,\theta}$.

3.3 Asymmetry over the Business Cycle

This section examines the way in which the elasticity of tax revenue with respect to the tax rate is likely to vary over the business cycle, and in particular how this depends on the degree of asymmetry, as measured by s. It proceeds by considering the cyclical pattern of a corporation's profits and losses as being represented as increases or decreases in θ around a trend value. The absolute size of the trend value of θ, which is likely to vary across firms, is not itself important. What matters is the behaviour of the component partial elasticities $\eta'_{T,\theta}$, $\eta'_{T,s}$, and $\eta'_{s,\theta}$ as θ moves upwards towards $\theta = 1$ and downwards, including $\theta \leq 0$ (above-trend and below-trend respectively). As a point of reference, the examples below initially consider the case where the behavioural response, $\eta_{\theta,t}$, is fixed; that is, it does not vary as θ varies over the cycle. This allows variations in the elasticity $\eta_{T,t}$ to be related directly to variations in the total elasticity, $\eta_{T,\theta}$, and hence to θ for alternative s, for specific assumptions about the partial elasticity $\eta'_{s,\theta}$.

As a preliminary exercise, Figure 3.2 plots $\eta_{T,\theta}$ against θ for alternative values of s, for the case where $\eta'_{s,\theta} = 0$ in (3.23). In this extreme case, $\eta_{T,\theta} = \eta'_{T,\theta}$ and equation (3.20) can be used. Consider the range $\theta > 0$ for which net profits are positive. It has been shown that $\eta_{T,\theta} = 1$ for all θ in the symmetric case of $s = 1$: this is the top horizontal line in the figure. For $s < 1$, $\eta_{T,\theta}$ clearly increases as θ increases but the profile becomes flatter for relatively higher values of θ. When $\theta = 0$, the value of $\eta_{T,\theta}$ is zero for all values of s, and Figure 3.2 shows that the further s is below 1 (the greater the asymmetry in the tax code), the smaller is the value of $\eta_{T,\theta}$: the profiles pivot around the origin and at the same time become flatter for lower s.

Given the general result in (3.18) that $\eta_{T,t} = 1 + \eta_{T,\theta}\eta_{\theta,t}$, these results show that, for a given (negative) behavioural response, $\eta_{\theta,t}$, greater loss asymmetry (lower s) results in smaller tax responsiveness; that is $\eta_{T,\theta}$ is lower and so $\eta_{T,t}$ is closer to 1. This effect is more pronounced the smaller is θ. Figure 3.2, also shows that for lower values of $\theta > 0$, the profiles of $\eta_{T,\theta}$ are closer together; hence the effect on $\eta_{T,\theta}$ of differences in s diminishes as θ tends to zero. As a result, the precise degree of asymmetry – as measured by s – becomes less relevant in determining the revenue elasticity.

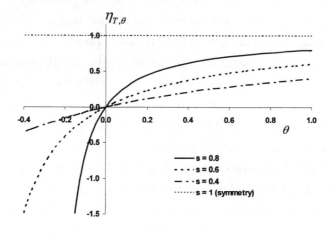

Figure 3.2: The Impact of Tax Loss Asymmetries

This latter point is important for estimates of behavioural responses in below-trend and above-trend situations. For the sake of illustration, assume that a trend value of θ is around 0.6. As the firm's performance moves above-trend (towards $\theta = 1$) this has little *additional* impact on the revenue elasticity $\eta_{T,\theta}$. However, as the firm's performance moves below trend (towards or below $\theta = 0$), the impact on $\eta_{T,\theta}$ becomes magnified, given the concavity of the profiles, which must all go through the origin. Thus, moving into recession has an asymmetric effect on $\eta_{T,\theta}$ compared with movements into boom periods for a given value of s. In other words, $\eta_{T,\theta}$ declines by more when moving into recession than it increases when moving into a boom. As a result, for a given behavioural response, $\eta_{\theta,t}$, the same asymmetric effects will be observed for $\eta_{T,t}$, as is clear from (3.23). Perhaps counter-intuitively, Figure 3.2 also suggests that this asymmetry, or nonlinearity, between above-trend and below-trend changes in $\eta_{T,\theta}$, is *less* when the asymmetry in the treatment of losses is greater (smaller s). This reflects the fact that $\eta_{T,\theta}$ is reduced so much at all values of θ when s is low (see, for example, the profile for $s = 0.4$ in Figure 3.2), that the impact of *differences in* θ becomes of limited importance.

Figure 3.2 also shows values of $\eta_{T,\theta}$ for negative values of θ; that is, when losses exceed profits. Negative θ values can be associated with a tax liability when s is sufficiently small such that $P > sL$, even though $P < L$. The Figure shows that the asymmetry between below-trend and above-trend effects is magnified further when $\theta < 0$ is considered. However, larger values of s (smaller asymmetries in loss treatment) are associated with larger deviations from $\eta_{T,\theta} = 1$ (the symmetric case), and $\eta_{T,\theta}$ also becomes negative. These negative values of $\eta_{T,\theta}$ arise from the fact that when $\theta < 0$ the firm has a positive tax liability associated with its negative net profits. Reducing the size of s, *ceteris paribus* increases the range of negative net profits over which the firm has a positive tax liability, so that there is a less pronounced effect on $\eta_{T,\theta}$ (it is closer to zero) at a given negative value of θ.

The above results assume somewhat unrealistically that $\eta'_{s,\theta} = 0$. When $\eta'_{s,\theta} \neq 0$, then s, θ, and $\eta'_{s,\theta}$ cannot be set independently. It is also not approporiate to assume that $\eta'_{s,\theta}$ is constant, since the implied relationship between logarithms of s and θ is incompatible with $\theta < 0$. Instead, assumed that $ds/d\theta$ is constant. Thus, rearranging the term in square brackets in (3.23) gives:

$$\eta_{T,\theta} = \left[\frac{\theta \left\{ s - (1 - \theta)ds/d\theta \right\}}{1 - s(1 - \theta)} \right] \qquad (3.24)$$

The importance of the additional effect on $\eta_{T,\theta}$ of allowing for the effect on s of changes in θ can be seen in Figure 3.3 which shows the relation between $\eta_{T,\theta}$ and θ, using (3.24) and setting $ds/d\theta = 0.1$.

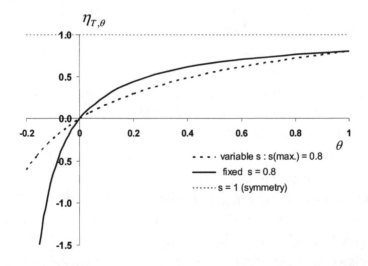

Figure 3.3: Loss Asymmetries with $ds/d\theta > 0$

To assist comparisons the maximum value of s, at $\theta = 1$ is set at $s = 0.8$, the equivalent fixed case also shown in the figure. This value of $ds/d\theta$ means that reductions in θ (increases in losses) modestly lower the firm's deductions rate, s, such that the present value of those losses, as tax deductions, falls. For example, with $ds/d\theta = 0.1$, and $s = 0.8$ at $\theta = 1$, s falls to 0.7 at $\theta = 0$. This shows that the concavity (to the x-axis) of the relationship between $\eta_{T,\theta}$ and θ when s is fixed, is reduced. This reflects the fact that as θ falls due to rising losses, fewer of those losses can be used to reduce tax liability when s is variable compared to s fixed. As a result the highly non-linear effect on $\eta_{T,\theta}$ generated by decreases in θ when s is fixed is ameliorated by an opposing effect due to decreased s. It can be shown, for this variable s case, that if the maximum s (at $\theta = 1$) is lower, the concavity of the relationship between θ and $\eta_{T,\theta}$ can even be reversed. For example, at maximum $s = 0.4$, and other parameters held at their values in Figure 3.3, the relationship becomes approximately linear. Of course, when there are no current losses, such that $\theta = 1$, a value of s close to, or equal to, 1 is to be expected (depending on past loss availability).

The intuition here is as follows. A tax-induced fall in θ may arise because losses are shifted into the tax jurisdiction when t rises. This has a direct effect of reducing tax revenue because loss deductions rise. However, the indirect effect is to reduce s which reduces loss deductions and raises tax revenue. Hence the negative behavioural effect on tax revenues of a rise in the tax rate due to the increase in losses declared for tax is compensated by a tendency for asymmetric loss restrictions to bind more tightly, which boosts tax revenue, *ceteris paribus*. The negative, non-linear 'tax base' effect is therefore compensated by an endogenous change in the effective rebate rate, $s_j t$.

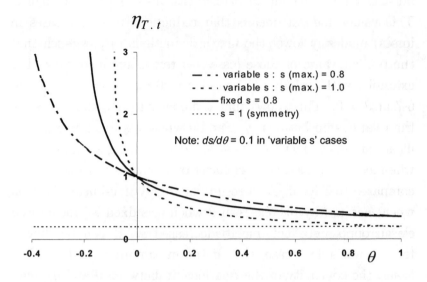

Figure 3.4: The Elasticity $\eta_{T,t}$; with $\eta_{\theta,t} = -0.8$

The tax revenue elasticity, $\eta_{T,t}$, is shown in Figure 3.4, for a behavioural response of $\eta_{\theta,t} = -0.8$. The symmetric ($s = 1$), and three asymmetric, cases are illustrated: $ds/d\theta = 0$, and $ds/d\theta = 0.1$, for $s(\text{max}) = 0.8$ and 1. This shows that in the case of symmetric treatment of losses, the elasticity, $\eta_{T,t}$, is flat at $1 + \eta_{T,\theta}\eta_{\theta,t} = 1 - 0.8 = 0.2$. However, the asymmetric treatment of losses causes the elasticity to exceed 0.2 for all values of θ and to fall sharply as θ increases. As with $\eta_{T,\theta}$, the $\eta_{T,t}$ elasticity falls more steeply as θ rises, at low values of θ (that is, in more severe recessions), when the asymmetric treatment of losses is less (that is, s closer to unity). However, the convexity (to the x-axis) of this relationship is reduced when $ds/d\theta \neq 0$, and with $s(\text{max})$ set at the equivalent fixed value of 0.8. Raising

s (max) to 1.0 has the opposite effect of increasing the degree of non-linearlity.

Consider the extreme right-hand side where $\theta = 1$, which implies that $\eta_{T,\theta} = \eta'_{T,\theta} = s$ and $\eta_{T,t} = 1 + s\eta_{\theta,t}$: hence the revenue elasticity is, as expected, closer to the symmetric case the greater is s. However, the profiles intersect at $\theta = 0$; $\eta_{T,\theta} = 1$, as shown in the figure. This can be seen from (3.24) to result from the fact that $\eta_{T,\theta} = 0$ if $\theta = 0$. Hence $\eta_{T,t} = 1 + \eta_{T,\theta}\eta_{\theta,t} = 1$ in all cases all the profiles shown in Figure 3.4 must intersect when $\eta_{T,t} = 1$. The revenue elasticity can thus exceed 1, to an extent depending on s, where losses are relatively high (that is, when θ is negative), the magnitude depending on the partial elasticity $\eta'_{s,\theta} > 0$. This reflects the fact that at low θ and/or s, the revenue-enhancing effect of tighter loss restrictions is sufficient to outweigh the revenue-depleting effect of increased losses ('real' or shifted into the tax jurisdiction) in response to the tax rate rise.

These results suggest that the elasticity of tax revenues with respect to changes in tax rates, $\eta_{T,t}$, (a variable commonly estimated in the empirical profit-shifting literature) can be expected in general to be higher (indicating a lower behavioural response) in regimes that involve greater asymmetries in the tax treatment of losses. This holds in both below-trend and above-trend situations. However, during recessions, when there are large losses, estimates of behavioural responses are likely to be especially sensitive to the precise combination of relative loss sizes, θ, and the degree of asymmetry, s.

The results obtained above have taken the value of the behavioural elasticity, $\eta_{\theta,t}$, as being constant for different values of θ. However, it may be that, faced with increasing difficulty of gaining tax deductions from their losses when θ is small, firms tend to increase their behavioural responsiveness to compensate; that is $\eta_{\theta,t}$ becomes more negative when $\eta_{T,\theta}$ is low during recessions. In the limit this could have the effect of keeping the term $\eta_{T,\theta}\eta_{\theta,t}$ in (3.19) constant over the cycle. The ability of firms to do this is likely to depend on the ease with which firms can adjust the amount of losses that they shift into or out of the tax jurisdiction in response to tax rate changes. To the extent that such adjustments can be made, the nonlinear profiles in Figures 3.2 to 3.4 provide measures of the size of adjustments that would be required to achieve 'full compensation' for the differential impact of loss asymmetries over the cycle. The evidence of Auerbach (2007), that there are sizeable cyclical fluctuations in US corporations' effective average tax rates, suggests that US firms are unable or unwilling to shift profits and losses sufficiently to prevent the cyclical impact of tax loss asymmetries from raising their effective tax rates during downturns.

3.4   Conclusions

Losses tend to be treated less generously than profits in the corporate tax codes of many countries. This typically means that, in present value terms, losses generate a lower tax rebate than the positive tax levied on equivalent sized profits. This asymmetry has two opposing effects on corporate tax liabilities when corporate losses increase. On the one hand increased losses give rise to a larger 'base' for tax rebates. On the other hand, the asymmetries of the tax code bind more tightly when losses are larger, which has the effect of pushing up the effective average tax rate. This chapter has considered the relevance of this phenomenon for estimates of companies' behavioural responses to changes in corporate tax rates. These responses involve shifting profits and losses into or out of the tax jurisdiction.

In order to make the effective tax rate applied to losses more transparent, an equivalent tax function facing a firm was specified having the same present value of tax revenue as the actual function but allowing for a partial rebate in each period, where appropriate. This function involved a measure of asymmetry equal to the present value of the period's losses as tax offsets, as a ratio of their nominal value.

It was shown that the response of tax revenue to a change in the tax rate, $\eta_{T,t}$, can be decomposed into the response, $\eta_{\theta,t}$, of the ratio of net-to-gross profits, θ, to the tax rate, t (a behavioural response), and the response of tax revenues to a change in the ratio of net-to-gross profits. The latter arises both directly, via a partial elasticity $\eta'_{T,\theta}$, and indirectly via changes in the impact of loss asymmetries, measured by the product of the partial elasticities, $\eta'_{T,s}$ and $\eta'_{s,\theta}$, which are determined by the tax code and firms' profit and loss situations. These latter responses 'translate' behavioural responses into tax revenue changes.

Asymmetries in the way losses are treated in the tax code reduce tax revenue responses to tax rate changes by reducing the sum of the direct and indirect effects, $\eta_{T,\theta} = \eta'_{T,\theta} + \eta'_{T,s}\eta'_{s,\theta}$, below unity, the value when there are no asymmetries. The size of the reduction increases as the asymmetry increases. This effect was found to be non-linear with respect to the economic cycle. It is disproportionately strong during recessionary periods, when losses are relatively large, but is dispoportionately weak during boom periods, when losses are small. These disproportionate recessionary effects are larger the smaller is the asymmetry.

Therefore behavioural responses of tax revenue to tax rate changes are likely to be smaller (that is, $\eta_{T,t}$ deviates less below unity) for tax regimes which impose greater constraints on loss use within the tax code and when these responses are measured during periods when corporate losses are abnormally high. However, when losses are abnormally low, *ceteris paribus* larger behavioural responses are likely to be observed.

Chapter 4

Taxes and Income Shifting

This chapter examines a number of different behavioural responses by companies to changes in the taxation of their profits in the home country. Such responses can take two forms. First, there are real responses, whereby activities are transferred to other tax jurisdictions. The second form of response involves income-shifting in which the location of economic activity is unchanged but the extent to which profits are declared in the home country changes. Here there is of course a significant role for transfer pricing; see Gresik (2001, pp. 808-811). In the context of personal income taxation, Feldstein (1995, 1999) introduced the concept of the elasticity of taxable income with respect to the retention rate (one minus the tax rate). Though this concept was initially proposed as a means of capturing real behavioural responses to tax reforms, Slemrod and Yitzhaki (2002) showed that the concept can be applied to any responses which cause the tax base to respond to exogenous changes in tax parameters.[1] The closely related concept of the elasticity of taxable profits with respect to the corporate tax rate is therefore central, and

---

[1] A convenient feature of the concept is that, under certain conditions, it provides valuable information about efficiency costs of taxation. For a recent review of evidence, see Saez *et al.* (2009). An introduction to the concept is provided in Creedy (2009).

is the focus of attention here.

The components of companies' responses are considered by decomposing this elasticity and it is argued that it is particularly important to distinguish between the responsiveness of gross profits and that of deductions allowable as profit off-sets. Where these deductions are related to the size of companies' profits, it is found that allowing for an endogenous, or automatic, response may be important for empirical estimates of firms' overall behavioural responses.

Income shifting arises where multinational companies can change the extent to which they declare their profits in different countries in response to differences in international profits taxation, without changing their real activities. Empirical estimates suggest that these shifting responses could be substantial; see, for example, studies by Hines and Rice (1994), Hines (1999), Grubert and Slemrod (1998), Bartelsman and Beetsma (2003) and Huizinga and Laeven (2007). In addition, as Markusen (2002) and Devereux and Hubbard (2003) have demonstrated, multinational firms' decisions regarding whether to locate real production facilities at home or abroad, and trade between locations, can be influenced by profit taxation; see also Feldstein *et al.* (eds) (1995). Real responses are not confined to multinational firms. They can also be expected for purely domestic firms because increases in tax rates reduce net-of-tax profits at the margin and so render some previously profitable production unprofitable. In some cases firms may change to non-corporate status where personal and corporate income tax regimes differ.

The present chapter begins by examining the elasticity for individual firms. However, from a policy point of view, it is important also to consider what happens to aggregate tax revenues. A second aim of the chapter is to consider the potential behaviour of the aggregate revenue elasticity with respect to the tax rate over the business cycle. In considering such dynamics, an important role is played by the asymmetric nature of the corporate tax system whereby losses do not give rise to a rebate, so that the use of loss pools over the cycle has a substantial influence. The implications of this asymmetry are investigated using a stylised dynamic process.

Section 4.1 defines and decomposes firms' behavioural responses. Section 4.2 considers the orders of magnitude of elasticities of tax paid with respect to the tax rate, for individual firms, using possible orders of magnitude of important components suggested by previous empirical studies. The potential behaviour over the business cycle of the aggregate tax revenue elasticity with respect to the tax rate is then examined in section 4.3.

4.1 Types of Behavioural Response

This section begins by defining alternative behavioural responses to corporate taxation, decomposing these into real responses, profit-shifting and deductions-shifting. The context is of a firm located in a home country, or tax jurisdiction, which may at some cost change its declared profits in that jurisdiction in response to a change in the home tax rate. This includes, but is not limited to, moving profits abroad which may or may not involve shifting some aspects of real economic activity. For comparative static purposes, tax rates abroad are assumed throughout to be independent of the tax rate in the home country, so that responses to a change in the home tax rate can be interpreted as responses to a change in the tax differential.

Subsection 4.1.1 begins by specifying the composition of taxable profits. Subsection 4.1.2 considers declared profits and deductions. Subsection 4.1.3 then decomposes the overall change in a firm's tax, in response to a change in the tax rate, into its various components. Subsection 4.1.4 considers the likely signs attached to the components.

4.1.1 Taxable Profits

For a single company, net taxable profits, P^T, are defined as the difference between gross profits declared for tax, P^*, and total deductions claimed against those profits, $D^* = D(P^*)$, so that:

$$P^T = P^* - D^* \tag{4.1}$$

The firm's tax liability, $T(P^*)$, is some function of P^T. In many countries this is a multi-step function, containing a number of rates and thresholds. However, within any range, tax liability can be expressed as an equivalent single-rate structure: in the context of personal income taxation, see Creedy and Gemmell (2006, p. 25). Furthermore, the vast majority of corporation tax is typically raised at a main or standard rate. Hence it is sufficient in what follows to consider a single rate structure:

$$\begin{aligned} T(P^*) &= 0 & \text{if } P^T \leq 0 \\ &= tP^T = t(P^* - D^*) & \text{if } P^T > 0 \end{aligned} \tag{4.2}$$

There may (as in some European Union countries) be some form of non-refundable tax credit, associated for example with research and development expenditure. In most cases it is possible to redefine such credits in terms of their deductions equivalent.

However, there may be special conditions governing when the credits can be claimed. Hence in what follows, the existence of credits is ignored.

There is clearly an asymmetry in the tax treatment of profits arising from the fact that losses do not give rise to a tax rebate, but instead are deductible against current or future positive profits within the corporation or group defined for tax purposes. This feature applies to the UK, the US and numerous other countries' corporate tax structures.[2] The implications of this kind of asymmetry for investment behaviour have been examined by Auerbach (1986), Devereux (1989), Altshuler and Auerbach (1990) and Edgerton (2007); see also Auerbach (2007). It will be seen below to have important implications in the present context.

For a firm with positive net taxable profits:

$$\frac{dT}{dt} = P^T + t\frac{dP^T}{dt} \tag{4.3}$$

where dP^T/dt measures the combined extent of real changes and profit shifting in response to the tax rate change. Dividing both sides by P^T and using the fact that $\frac{dT}{P^T dt} = \frac{t dT}{T dt}$ gives:

$$\eta_{T,t} = 1 + \eta_{P^T,t} \tag{4.4}$$

where in general $\eta_{x,y} = (dx/dy)(y/x)$ denotes the elasticity of x with respect to y. Thus the main elasticity of interest is the elasticity, $\eta_{P^T,t}$, of net taxable profit with respect to the tax rate.

---

[2]For example, in the UK system as discussed in further detail in Part III below, a current loss under one profit schedule may be offset against a current profit under some, but not all, other schedules. Thus a firm's ability to utilise its losses immediately can depend on the schedular characteristics of its profits and losses. Further conditions apply to firms which form part of a group. See Agúndez (2006) for discussion of intra-group loss-offsetting among European firms.

It is this elasticity that is decomposed, and examined further, below.

4.1.2 Declared Profits and Deductions

Allowing for behavioural responses requires the extent to which profits and deductions are declared in the home tax jurisdiction to be specified. At this stage the use of different 'schedules' for different sources of income is ignored. Define θ_p as the proportion of total gross profits, P, which are declared at home, so that, where time subscripts are omitted for convenience:

$$P^* = \theta_p P \qquad (4.5)$$

Similarly, let θ_d denote the proportion of total deductions which are declared at home, and let E denote qualifying expenditures eligible as offsets against declared profit. These include capital allowances arising from investment expenditures and accumulated losses. A proportion, s, of these qualifying expenditures can be deducted, so that declared deductions, D^*, are:

$$D^* = s\theta_d E \qquad (4.6)$$

The deductions rate, s, is analogous to the term used by Devereux and Hubbard (2003, p. 473) to describe a 'factor which reflects the generosity of the provision for depreciation'. In the present chapter, s represents the generosity of the tax code regarding all qualifying expenditures, not just those on capital. To the extent that a firm's total profits or qualifying expenditures change in response to changes in taxes, whilst keeping constant the extent to which they are declared for tax at home, these may be regarded as real. Alternatively, where total profits or qualifying expenditures remain unchanged but the proportion declared at home alters, some profit or deductions shifting can be considered to have occurred.

Equation (4.1) can be rewritten as:

$$P^T = \theta_p P - s\theta_d E \tag{4.7}$$

It is convenient to let α denote the ratio of declared profits to the tax base, so that:

$$\alpha = \frac{P^*}{P^T} = \frac{\theta_p P}{P^T} \tag{4.8}$$

Hence, using (4.7):

$$\begin{aligned}
\alpha &= 1 + \frac{s\theta_d E}{P^T} \\
&= \left\{ 1 - \left(\frac{s\theta_d}{\theta_p} \right) \left(\frac{E}{P} \right) \right\}^{-1} = \left\{ 1 - \left(\frac{D^*}{P^*} \right) \right\}^{-1} \tag{4.9}
\end{aligned}$$

and α is strictly greater than one as long as there are some declared deductions; that is $D^* > 0$.

Key ratios used in later sections to examine the cyclical properties of behavioural responses to tax changes are the ratios of qualifying expenditures to gross profits, E/P, or the ratio of declared deductions to declared profits, D^*/P^*, where the latter is more readily observable in taxpayer data. These ratios can be expected to vary over the cycle as increasing or decreasing losses respectively raise or lower E and D^*, relative to the profit variables, P and P^*. Equation (4.9) shows that α varies positively with these ratios.

4.1.3 Behavioural Elasticity Components

To identify the impact of real and shifting deductions responses to tax rate changes the elasticity of net taxable profits in (4.4) can be expressed in terms of its components. Thus, differentiating (4.7) with respect to t, and using the definition of α in (4.9), it can be shown that:

$$\eta_{PT,t} = \alpha \left\{ \eta_{\theta_p,t} + \eta_{P,t} \right\} - (\alpha - 1) \left\{ \eta_{\theta_d,t} + \eta_{E,t} \right\} \qquad (4.10)$$

Equation (4.10) provides the basic decomposition of the elasticity of taxable profit with respect to the tax rate for a single firm. The first term in curly brackets, $\left\{ \eta_{\theta_p,t} + \eta_{P,t} \right\}$, measures profit responses while the second term, $\left\{ \eta_{\theta_d,t} + \eta_{E,t} \right\}$, measures deductions responses. The four component elasticities capture the four basic behavioural responses and are summarised in Table 4.1.

Table 4.1: Responses to a Tax Change

Income shifting		
Profit shifting:	$\theta_p = \theta_p(t)$	$d\theta_p/dt < 0$
Deductions shifting:	$\theta_d = \theta_d(t,s)$	$d\theta_d/dt > 0$
Real responses		
Real profit response:	$P = P(t)$	$dP/dt < 0$
Real deductions response:	$E = E(t,s)$	$dE/dt0$

The extent to which firms shift profits or deductions out of the home tax net is likely to depend on the relative costs of each. For example, it may be easier to hide profits than to inflate deductions, depending on the specification of the tax code, the extent and form of enforcement activity, and the available evasion and avoidance facilities.[3]

---

[3] Grubert and Slemrod (1998) suggested that firms which create opportunities for real profit responses, for example by setting up foreign subsidiaries, are likely to find it easier to engage in profit-shifting; indeed the two may be joint decisions. As a result it might be expected that firms with larger values of $\eta_{P,t}$ are more likely to have larger values of $\eta_{\theta_p,t}$.

4.1.4 Expected Signs

In general the expected directions of change are indicated in the final column of Table 4.1. These sign expectations assume that substitution effects dominate any income effects: this accords with Gruber and Saez's (2002) finding that compensated and uncompensated taxable income elasticities are similar. Furthermore, the overwhelming majority of taxable income elasticity studies since Feldstein (1995, 1999) find the overall elasticity with respect to the retention rate to be positive.

Even if the elasticity terms on the right-hand side of (4.10) were to take similar values across firms, differences in α would ensure that $\eta_{PT,t}$ varies. In particular, as is evident from (4.9), firms with a larger deductions base have a higher α, *ceteris paribus*, and hence a larger absolute $\eta_{PT,t}$.[4] As a result, profit-making firms with a recent history of losses (or profit-making members of a group with large losses elsewhere) and firms with large capital allowances can be expected, *ceteris paribus*, to have stronger negative responses to a tax change. For firms declaring a current loss or zero profit, $\eta_{PT,t}$ is of course zero.

The sign of $\eta_{E,t}$ in (4.10) is complicated by the fact that, to the extent that some qualifying expenditures are related to profits, there may be some automatic response of deductions to tax-induced changes in profits declared at home. For example, suppose a firm transfers production abroad in response to a tax change, so that some profits previously obtained at home are now earned abroad. The associated investment which shifts abroad, previously deductible from profits declared at home, are

---

[4]The term 'larger absolute' is preferred here to 'smaller (more negative)'. Similarly, the term 'smaller absolute' is preferred to 'larger (less negative)'.

no longer deductible. This automatic response response can be expressed as the elasticity, η_{E,P^*}.

Furthermore, define the partial elasticity, $\eta'_{E,t}$, which captures the extent to which firms generate additional qualifying expenditures independently of declared profits, that is, the elasticity of E with respect to t, when P^* is held constant. This can be referred to as an 'autonomous' elasticity. The elasticity, $\eta_{E,t}$, can therefore be decomposed as:

$$\eta_{E,t} = \eta'_{E,t} + \left(\eta_{E,P^*}\right)\left(\eta_{P^*,t}\right) \tag{4.11}$$

For example, where enforcement of tax rules make it easier for firms to generate additional deductions via real changes to qualifying expenditures, rather than shift profits or deductions abroad, $\eta'_{E,t}$ (and hence $\eta_{E,t}$) could be high relative to $\eta_{\theta_p,t}$ or $\eta_{\theta_d,t}$ in equation (4.10).

In general the sign of $\eta_{E,t}$ is ambiguous. Consider the components on the right-hand side of (4.11). Although it is likely that $\eta'_{E,t} > 0$ and $\eta_{P^*,t} < 0$, the sign of the automatic response, η_{E,P^*}, depends on the type of qualifying expenditure and whether changes in P^* arise from changes in total profits, P, or changes in profit-shifting, θ_p. It might also be expected that where the tax code causes a greater automatic response, that is, a larger absolute value of η_{E,P^*}, firms may adopt a larger autonomous shifting response, $\eta'_{E,t}$, to compensate. Where, for example, a tax rise leads to more investment overseas, firms may attempt to compensate for the loss of capital allowances at home by shifting other deductions into the home tax jurisdiction where they have a greater tax offsetting value.

The automatic response elasticity η_{E,P^*} captures the extent to which, for given s and θ_d, claimed deductions change as declared profits change. This is affected both by changes in firms' economic circumstances and by tax rules. In a situation of steady-state or trend growth, a value of $\eta_{E,P*}$ equal or close to unity might be expected, otherwise deductions would become a persistently increasing or declining fraction of declared profits over the long-run. However, away from the steady-state, $\eta_{E,P*}$ may be greater than unity. This could arise when, following a recession, deductions rise faster than profits. Alternatively it may be less than unity, or even negative, during booms when past losses are exhausted and profits grow faster than deductions.

It is often easier to observe declared deductions, D^*, rather than the associated qualifying expenditures, E, in taxpayer data. Hence it is useful to consider the equivalent of (4.10) expressed in terms of declared deductions, D^* and declared profits, P^*. First, define the elasticity, $\eta_{D^*,t}$, using, as in (4.11):

$$\eta_{D^*,t} = \eta'_{D^*,t} + \left(\eta_{D^*,P^*}\right)\left(\eta_{P^*,t}\right) \qquad (4.12)$$

where, as above, a prime on the elasticity indicates that P^* is held constant; that is, $\eta'_{D^*,t} > 0$ is the autonomous elasticity of declared deductions with respect to the tax rate, for given declared profits. It captures any tendency for higher tax rates to encourage increased deductions *ceteris paribus* via either real or shifting responses.

Then, differentiating $P^T = \theta_p P - D^*$ gives:

$$\eta_{P^T,t} = \alpha\eta_{P^*,t} - (\alpha - 1)\eta_{D^*,t} \qquad (4.13)$$

where $\eta_{P^*,t} = \eta_{\theta_p,t} + \eta_{P,t}$. Using (8.1), equation (4.13) can be rewritten as:

$$\eta_{P^T,t} = \left\{\alpha - (\alpha - 1)\eta_{D^*,P^*}\right\}\eta_{P^*,t} - (\alpha - 1)\eta'_{D^*,t} \qquad (4.14)$$

This expression reveals three effects on the tax base elasticity, $\eta_{PT,t}$. The elasticities $\eta_{P*,t}$ and $\eta'_{D*,t}$ are the combined real and shifting responses for declared profits and autonomous deductions respectively, and $\eta_{D*,P*}$ is the endogenous or automatic deductions response.[5]

Both profits and deductions have direct negative effects on $\eta_{PT,t}$. That is, the responses of both to increases in tax rates (profit outflow, deductions inflow) serve to increase the absolute value of $\eta_{PT,t}$. However, there is an additional indirect effect of a profit outflow, namely the loss of some deductions, captured by $\eta_{D*,P*}$, that otherwise could be claimed against declared profit: this reduces the absolute value of $\eta_{PT,t}$. From the first curly brackets in (4.14) the direct effect dominates if:

$$\eta_{D*,P*} < \frac{\alpha}{\alpha - 1} \qquad (4.15)$$

This inequality identifies the conditions under which a reduction in declared profits in response to a tax increase (whether via real or shifting effects) raises or lowers tax liabilities, relative to the case where $\eta_{P*,t} = 0$. If condition (4.15) holds, a negative profit response to the increased tax rate generates a lower tax liability than when there is no response. However, where condition (4.15) does not hold, the loss of deductions which could be used to offset profits, when declared profits are reduced by a tax rate rise, would have a net effect of increasing firms' tax liabilities. In this case, firms have incentives to shift profits *into* the tax jurisdiction when the tax rate rises due to the value of associated deductions.

In general, there is no reason to expect (4.15) to hold since it depends on how the endogenous response of deductions to

---

[5]In a steady-state, $\eta_{E,P*} = 1$ with $\eta_{D*,P*} = 1$.

profit *changes* compares with the relative *size* of deductions to profits. Both could be determined by different characteristics of a corporate tax system.[6]

4.2 Illustrative Examples

To illustrate orders of magnitude for the elasticity, $\eta_{PT,t}$, for a single firm or group, it is necessary to consider possible values for the component elasticities. Subsection 4.2.1 first reviews estimates from empirical studies which provide a guide to orders of magnitude relevant to the UK corporate tax system. Based on these estimates, a set of benchmark parameters are described in subsection 4.2.2, after which subsection 4.2.3 presents numerical results.

4.2.1 Estimates of Response Parameters

Various estimates of responses are available in the empirical literature which can be used to guide choices in producing illustrative examples and simulations reported below. Income-shifting responses were estimated for samples of multinational corporations by Bartelsman and Beetsma (2003), Grubert and Slemrod (1998) and Hines and Rice (1994). Using OECD country-level data on the share of labour income in value added, Bartelsman and Beetsma (2003) estimated pure profit shifting for OECD countries on average. Their central estimate of profit shifting is that about 65 per cent of additional revenue following a tax rate rise leaks abroad.

---

[6]For example, the use of past and current losses as profits offsets tends to generate a relationship between deductions and profits. However, the introduction of other deductions which may be unrelated to profits, or changes in qualifying expenditures, can raise the level of total deductions allowable against profits.

Thus the elasticity of declared revenue with respect to the tax rate is around 0.35. From (8.9), since $\eta_{PT,t} = \eta_{T,t} - 1$, the implied tax base elasticity is -0.65. Bartelsma and Beetsma (2003) obtained UK parameter estimates close to the OECD average. This may be regarded as an estimate of the profit-shifting component, $\alpha\eta_{\theta_p,t} - (\alpha - 1)\eta_{\theta_d,t}$, rather than of the total real-plus-shifting response. By focussing only on income-shifting responses Bartelsma and Beetsma argued that their estimates could be regarded as lower bounds. More detailed recent estimates for European multinationals, from Huizinga and Laeven (2007), are somewhat smaller for the UK than those derived from the Bartelsman and Beetsma results. Huizinga and Laeven (2007) estimate a semi-elasticity of reported profits with respect to the top statutory tax rate of around 1.1 for the UK, which implies an elasticity of -0.33, assuming a 30 per cent corporate tax rate.[7]

Grubert and Slemrod (1998) focused on profit shifting to Puerto Rico by US multinationals, allowing for both real foreign investment and profit shifting to tax havens. Though estimates of an elasticity are not readily derivable, their results confirm that substantial real-plus-profit-shifting responses by US multinationals was mainly motivated by the profit-shifting opportunities which the real foreign investment provides.

Hines and Rice (1994) examined aggregate 1982 country-level data for reported non-financial profits of US parents and affiliates with investments in tax havens and other foreign countries. They report that a 1 percentage point higher tax rate reduces re-

---

[7]However, the Huizinga and Laeven semi-elasticities are based on profits data in commercial accounts and are not necessarily equivalent to the elasticity measured here which relates to net taxable profits.

ported profits by 3 per cent. Across such a wide-ranging sample of countries, the corporate tax rate is likely to vary. An average of around 30 per cent implies an elasticity around -1; a 15 per cent tax rate implies an elasticity around -0.5. The Hines–Rice elasticity probably includes both real and profit-shifting responses and so approximates $\eta_{PT,t}$.

4.2.2 Benchmark Parameters

This subsection considers a set of benchmark parameters for numerical examples. The following examples assume a steady-state, for which $\eta_{E,P*} = 1$ with $\eta_{D*,P*} = 1$, so that:

$$\eta_{PT,t} = \left(\eta_{\theta_p,t} + \eta_{P,t}\right) - (\alpha - 1)\left\{\eta_{\theta_d,t} + \eta'_{E,t}\right\} \qquad (4.16)$$

Hence, in the steady state, the value of $\eta_{PT,t}$ depends on α and the four elasticity components in (4.16). These elasticities determine the real responses of profits, P, and qualifying expenditures, E, and of the shifting parameters, θ_p and θ_d. The illustrations below also set $s = 1$. The examples report values of $\eta_{PT,t}$ as the ratio E/P varies. Hence the value of α also varies as shown in equation (4.9) above.

Table 4.2 shows the assumed values of the four elasticity components and the declared proportions, θ_p and θ_d, required to calculate $\alpha - 1$ in (4.16). It might be expected that these parameters cannot be chosen independently by firms. For example, if it becomes more costly to shift further increments of profits abroad, then $\eta_{\theta_p,t}$ and $\eta_{\theta_d,t}$ may become smaller as θ_p and θ_d are reduced. However, the numerical illustrations examine individual parameter changes holding all others constant.

The benchmark case assumes a 5 per cent real profit response to changing tax rates, but alternatives of 10 per cent and 20 per

Table 4.2: Benchmark Parameter Values

	Elasticity	Benchmark	Alternatives
Profit shifting	$\eta_{\theta_p,t}$	−0.375	−0.625
Deductions shifting	$\eta_{\theta_d,t}$	0.25	0.5
Real profit response	$\eta_{P,t}$	−0.05	−0.1, −0.2
Real deductions response	$\eta'_{E,t}$	0.05	0.1, 0.2
Proportion of P declared	θ_p	0.8	0.6
Proportion of D declared	θ_d	0.8	0.6
Deductions rate	s	1.0	0.8, 0.6

cent are also examined. Comparable positive values are used for the autonomous real deductions response, $\eta'_{E,t}$. With $s = 1$ and for a given θ_d, the response of qualifying expenditures is the same as that for declared deductions. This response is referred to as autonomous or 'discretionary' to distinguish it from the automatic deductions response.

A benchmark elasticity of $\eta_{\theta_p,t} = -0.375$ is assumed, with deductions shifting assumed to be slightly more difficult such that $\eta_{\theta_d,t} = 0.25$.[8] Using $E/P = 0.5$ gives a value of $\alpha = 2$ from (4.9) with $s = 1$ and $\theta_d/\theta_p = 1$. This yields a benchmark total shifting elasticity of $\eta_{\theta_p,t} - (\alpha - 1)\eta_{\theta_d,t} = -0.625$.

These illustrative values should not be interpreted as representing 'average' responses, since many firms' responses could be expected to be very small or zero. However they serve to illustrate the responsiveness properties of those firms with more substantial behavioural reactions to tax changes.

---

[8]If profit-shifting is driven by changes in the tax rate differential between home and overseas tax jurisdictions, the assumed precentage change in the home tax rate is small compared with the percentage change in the differential. For example if the home rate falls from 25 per cent to 23 per cent (a −8 per cent change) but the relevant overseas rate remains at, say, 35 per cent, the differential has changed by 20 per cent (from 10 per cent to 12 per cent). Thus a relatively large response to a relatively small change in the home tax rate may not be so surprising.

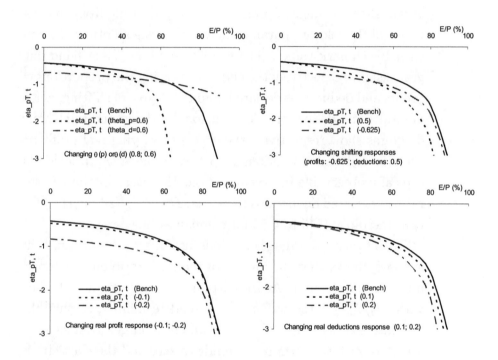

Figure 4.1: Relationship between $\eta_{PT,t}$ and E/P: Individual Firms

4.2.3   Numerical Results

Some numerical results are shown in Figure 4.1, where each of the four diagrams shows the elasticity $\eta_{PT,t}$ on the vertial axis and the size of qualifying expenditures relative to total profits, E/P, on the horizontal axis, expressed as a percentage. Each diagram shows a range of profiles for $\eta_{PT,t}$, resulting from changes in one of the relevant parameters while leaving all others fixed at their benchmark values. The top left-hand and right-hand diagrams show respectively the effects of varying the proportions of profits and deductions declared, and the degree of shifting, again of profits and deductions. The bottom left-hand and right-hand diagrams show respectively the effects of varying real profit responses and real deductions responses. The E/P ratio is not typically observable in taxpayer data. However, for the UK the ratio of declared deductions to profits, $D^*/P^* = (s\theta_d/\theta_p)\,(E/P)$, is in the range 0.45 to 0.56 for companies in aggregate.[9]

To interpret the diagrams, it is useful to bear in mind, as stressed above, that the impact of the E/P ratio on $\eta_{PT,t}$ operates via changes in α. At the extremes, as E/P tends to 1, then with $s\theta_d/\theta_p = 1$ the weight $\alpha - 1$ tend to infinity, so that the absolute elasticity, $\eta_{PT,t}$ becomes infinitely large. And as E/P tends to zero, the term $\alpha - 1$ tends to zero and the elasticity is determined solely by the first two profit-related terms in (4.16). In all the diagrams it is clear that the E/P ratio has important nonlinear effects on the overall behavioural elasticity, $\eta_{PT,t}$.

The top left-hand and bottom right-hand side diagrams of

---

[9]In the UK, data on all companies (excluding Life Assurance and North Sea Oil companies) over 1997–98 to 2003–04 show that the ratio of all deductions (excluding a small amount of tax credits), to gross declared profits, ranges from a low of 0.46 in 1998–99 to a high of 0.56 in 2002–03.   see http://www.hmrc.gov.uk/stats/corporate_tax/table11_2.pdf.

Figure 4.1 reveal that changes in θ_p, θ_d or $\eta'_{E,t}$ cause the benchmark profile to rotate, around a value at $E/P = 0$, whilst changes in $\eta_{P,t}$ cause the benchmark profile to shift (the bottom left-hand diagram). The top right-hand diagram also reveals that changes in the shifting elasticities have differing effects on the overall elasticity. An increase in the absolute value of $\eta_{\theta_p,t}$ causes the profile to shift downwards whilst an increase in $\eta_{\theta_d,t}$ causes the profile to rotate clockwise. This difference reflects the fact that the impact of $\eta_{\theta_d,t}$ on the overall elasticity is affected by $\alpha - 1$, whereas this is irrelevant to the impact of changes in $\eta_{\theta_p,t}$.

These illustrations show how differences in α can affect observed profit and deductions responses. However, by maintaining $\eta_{E,P*} = 1$, or equivalently, $\eta_{D*,P*} = 1$, they cannot demonstrate the endogenous impact on deductions of changes in declared profits. This aspect is likely to be important when considering behavioural responses at different points in the economic cycle, and is examined in the next section.

4.3 Responses over the Business Cycle

This section considers how the endogenous response of deductions to changes in declared profits, $\eta_{D*,P*}$, might change over the cycle as, for example, the ratio of losses to profits varies. This can translate into variations in $\eta_{PT,t}$ over the cycle as shown in equation (4.14). The resulting cyclical pattern observed for $\eta_{PT,t}$ also depends on any cyclical changes in the behavioural response elasticities. These might reasonably be thought of as fairly stable over the cycle, though firms may seek to increase their autonomous behavioural responses when endogenous responses otherwise restrict their ability to shift profits or deductions. Evidence for the US, reported by Auerbach(2007), suggests that, in aggregate, companies' effective average rates of corporate tax rise during recessions in association with increasing losses. Thus, if companies do indeed engage in profit shifting or loss shifting, these responses appear to be insufficient to counteract fully the impact of exogenous profit and loss cycles.

In this section it is convenient to work with the elasticity of taxable profits with respect to declared profits, $\eta_{P^T,P*}$ rather than the equivalent deductions elasticity, $\eta_{D*,P*}$. Differentiating equation (4.1):

$$\frac{dP^T}{dP^*} = 1 - \frac{dD^*}{dP^*}$$

and the two elasticities are related as follows:

$$\eta_{P^T,P*} = \alpha - (\alpha - 1)\eta_{D*,P*} \tag{4.17}$$

where, as previously, $\alpha = P^*/P^T$. That is, the two elasticities in (4.17) differ only by a factor due to the relative size of declared profits and deductions. Substituting (4.17) into (4.14) then gives:

$$\eta_{P^T,t} = \eta_{P^T,P*}\eta_{P*,t} - (\alpha - 1)\eta'_{D*,t} \tag{4.18}$$

Hence, if it is reasonable to assume that the behavioural elasticities, $\eta_{P*,t}$ and $\eta'_{D*,t}$ are relatively stable over the business cycle, the overall tax revenue response, $\eta_{P^T,t}$, can be expected to follow a similar (but inverse) cycle to $\eta_{P^T,P*}$ (since $\eta_{P*,t} < 0$). However, $\alpha - 1$ in (4.18) is also likely to be cyclical, as the ratio of deductions to profits changes.

Since interest here is in the effect of loss asymmetries, this section focusses on loss-related deductions only, which are likely to be the main cyclically-related deduction. Capital allowances are the other main deduction in the UK system. To the extent that investment is related to current profits, these would tend to be pro-cyclical. However empirical data do not suggest a clear cyclical pattern. However, in examining the cyclical behaviour of $\eta_{PT,P*}$ it is clearly of little interest to consider only firms that are persistently in either profit or loss (for whom $\eta_{PT,P*}$ is persistently 1 and 0 respectively) but to allow for firms that cycle between positive declared profits and losses. In fact the key dynamic properties of $\eta_{PT,P*}$ can readily be illustrated using just two firms, each of which is taxed independently and obtains profits from just one source. This is equivalent to assuming that there is full flexibility in using losses from different sources in different time periods, with all losses fully deductible against any current positive declared profits. Thus $s = 1$ in (4.6) above. In a full treatment, allowing for many firms, the aggregate equivalent of $\eta_{PT,P*}$ across all firms depends in a complex way on the changing distribution of profits over time and the use, including sharing of losses and other deductions. In Part IV below, a microsimulation model is used to examine this aspect for the UK. The model incorporates a number of the UK loss asymmetries, such as the limitations of group loss sharing.

With more than one firm it is necessary to consider the aggregate elasticity of taxable profits across both firms with respect to the tax rate, and its potential variation over the business cycle. Using Ω to denote the aggregate equivalent of η, it can be shown that $\Omega_{PT,P*}$ is a taxable profit share-weighted average of the individual elasticities:

$$\Omega_{P^T,P^*} = \sum_j \eta_{P^T,P^*} \left(\frac{P_j^T}{P^T}\right) \qquad (4.19)$$

where, in the present illustration, there are $j = 1, 2$ firms.

Let gross declared profits in period i for firm j be $P_{i,j}^*$; positive profits are denoted by $P_{i,j}^+ = \max\left(P_{i,j}^*, 0\right)$ and losses are $P_{i,j}^- = \max\left(-P_{i,j}^*, 0\right)$. If $L_{i,j}$ is firm j's loss pool in period i, carried over from the previous period, the losses available to be used as deductions in period i are thus $L_{i,j}^D = L_{i,j} + P_{i,j}^-$. Hence taxable profit for each firm is:

$$P_{i,j}^T = \max\left(P_{i,j}^+ - L_{i,j}^D, 0\right) \qquad (4.20)$$

and the loss pool carried forward to the next period is:

$$L_{i,j+1} = L_{i,j}^D - \min\left(P_{i,j}^+, L_{i,j}^D\right) \qquad (4.21)$$

Suppose that there is no trend growth in profits, but $P_{i,j}^*$ follows a similar cycle for each firm, described by a sine wave. An exogenous cycle in gross profits, P_j, rather than declared profits, P_j^*, is perhaps more appropriate but would require explicit modelling of profit shifting, $\theta_{p,j}$, over the cycle. For the purpose of the present illustration it is convenient to treat $\theta_{p,j}$ and P_j similarly. Hence, if A is the amplitude of the cycle and W is its wavelength, the time stream is given by:

$$P_{i,j}^* = A \sin\left(\frac{2\pi (i - 1)}{W}\right) + d_j \qquad (4.22)$$

where d_j is a shift parameter for each firm, determining the profit levels at central points of the cycle, such as $i = 1, 11, 21, ...$

Suppose that firm 1 is such that, over the business cycle, profit always remains positive. As explained above, in this simple context the individual elasticity, denoted by $\eta_{P_1^T,P_1^*}$, and measured as $\left(P_{i,j}^T - P_{i-1,j}^T\right)/P_{i-1,j}^T$ divided by $\left(P_{i,j}^* - P_{i-1,j}^*\right)/P_{i-1,j}^*$ for $i = 1$, is always equal to 1. But firm 2 experiences losses during some of the 'depression' periods. Profiles of gross and taxable profit for firm 2 are shown in Figure 4.2. The values were obtained using a wavelength of $W = 20$, an amplitude of 12, and shift parameters of $d_1 = 30$ and $d_2 = 4$. Once gross profit becomes negative, it is clear that taxable profit is zero. But once the firm begins to make positive profits again, the loss pool built up during the periods of negative profits can be used to keep $P_2^T = 0$. Hence where the dashed line, indicating P_2^T, in Figure 4.2 follows the horizontal axis, it must be the case that over this period, $\eta_{P_2^T,P_2^*} = 0$. Hence the aggregate elasticity Ω_{P^T,P^*} must be less than 1.

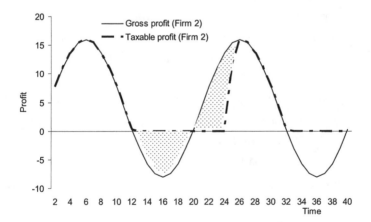

Figure 4.2: Gross and Taxable Profit Profiles for Firm 2

Eventually, as the loss pool of firm 2 moves towards exhaustion, there is a period during which taxable profit is positive but less than gross profit, as the last of the loss pool is used. In the example in Figure 4.2 this affects the individual, and hence aggregate, elasticity over two periods. Moving into positive taxable profit the individual elasticity is infinitely large, and then moving from the period when taxable profit is smaller than gross profit to that when they are equal (when the loss pool has been exhausted), the elasticity is greater than 1. In aggregate terms, taxable profit is growing faster than gross profit and hence the aggregate elasticity must exceed 1. In Figure 4.2 the shaded area between the horizontal axis and the profile of negative gross profit represents the loss pool built up during the depression. This must be equal to the subsequent shaded area above the horizontal axis. After this period, when gross and taxable profits move together for both firms, the aggregate elasticity Ω_{P^T,P^*} must again be 1.

The profiles of aggregate taxable and gross profits are shown in Figure 4.3. The dashed line, showing aggregate taxable profit, simply follows the gross (and taxable) profit of firm 1 during the period when firm 2 makes losses, and also in subsequent periods when firm 2 is able to keep its taxable profit equal to zero. Taxable profit thereafter moves up sharply to follow aggregate gross profit. When the two aggregate profiles are identical, then clearly $\Omega_{P^T,P^*} = 1$. When firm 2 has no taxable profit, $\Omega_{P^T,P^*} < 1$, and for the period when firm 2 moves from zero taxable profit to $0 < P^T < P^*$, the (two) individual elasticities are such that in aggregate $\Omega_{P^T,P^*} > 1$.

The elasticity profile is shown in Figure 4.4, where Ω_{P^T,P^*} is measured on the right vertical axis. This diagram also shows

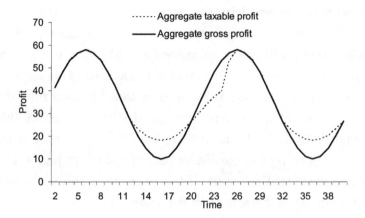

Figure 4.3: Aggregate Gross and Taxable Profits Over the Business Cycle

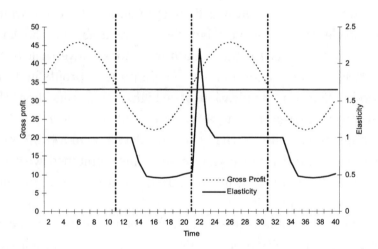

Figure 4.4: The Aggregate Elasticity of Taxable Profit with Respect to Gross Profit

the profile of aggregate gross profit, measured on the left vertical axis, so that the elasticity can easily be related to the business cycle. The horizontal and vertical lines drawn through the aggregate gross profit sine wave mark the mid-points of the cycles. As discussed above, the profile of the elasticity, $\Omega_{PT,P*}$, is horizontal until firm 2 begins to make a loss. It then dips down below 1 until firm 2 moves into positive taxable profit, when the aggregate elasticity has a sharp spike before settling back to $\Omega_{PT,P*} = 1$ during the remaining part of the boom period of the business cycle and the start of the depression period up to the point where firm 2 starts to make losses again.

The question then arises of how the profile of the elasticity $\Omega_{PT,P*}$ is affected by the amplitude of the business cycle. Figure 4.5 compares two business cycles. The solid line is the relatively low amplitude cycle, for which the previous results were obtained. The dashed line represents a cycle for which the wavelength is the same but the variation around the zero-growth positions is greater in both directions. Nevertheless, by construction, firm 1 continues to obtain positive profits in every period. The first implication of a higher amplitude must be that firm 2 moves into negative profits at an earlier point in the depression phase of the cycle and does not move into positive profits until later in the boom. This, combined with the fact that the loss pool built up during the negative profit periods is larger than with the lower amplitude cycle, means that the elasticity profile is less than 1 for longer. The subsequent spike in the elasticity profile is also greater. The two profiles are compared in Figure 4.6.

These results demonstrate that the asymmetry in the tax function's treatment of losses, compared with positive profits,

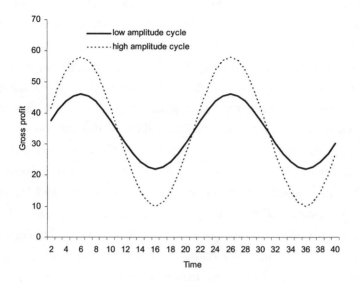

Figure 4.5: Low and High Amplitude Business Cycles

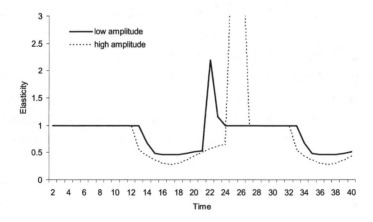

Figure 4.6: Elasticity Profiles for High and Low Amplitude Business Cycles

implies that over the business cycle the variation in the aggregate elasticity $\Omega_{PT,P*}$ itself displays an asymmetric pattern. During part of the boom period the elasticity is unity but during the depression it moves below 1 as soon as firm 2 makes losses. This is followed by a brief period when the elasticity exceeds unity, before it again equals 1. A higher amplitude of the cycle cannot raise the elasticity above 1 during the relevant periods, although the extent of the 'spike' above 1 is greater and the extent of the movement below 1 is greater. From equation (4.18), this means that the elasticity $\Omega_{T,t}$ is relatively high during depressions, when $\Omega_{PT,P*} < 1$, and relatively flat and low during the phase where $\Omega_{PT,P*} = 1$. That is, the relatively low endogenous response of taxable profits to gross profits during depressions, contributes towards a higher value of $\Omega_{T,t}$, implying a smaller behavioural response of tax revenue to the tax rate. (Recall $\Omega_{T,t} = 1$ in the absence of any behavioural response; see equation (4.4).

This simple model considers just two firms. The introduction of additional complexity arising from a distribution of firms does not affect the fundamental 'asymmetry' results. However, the existence of more firms moving into and out of losses at different phases of the business cycle must lead to a smoothing of the elasticity profile (rather than, for example, the sharp drop below unity when firm 2 begins to make losses) and a longer period during which the elasticity is above unity. The asymmetry over the business cycle nevertheless remains. This is because of the fact that the use of losses as deductions is relatively unimportant in above-trend growth, when aggregate losses are relatively small, but becomes particularly important in below-trend growth when losses are larger on average. This, in turn arises because the taxable profit distribution is effectively truncated at zero, unlike the gross profit distribution. Thus, large losses both generate additional deductions and simultaneously limit the ability of firms to claim them, until positive profits return, or they can be shared with group partners in profit.

Empirical evidence on the impact on corporate tax revenues of the asymmetry modelled in this chapter suggests that corporate tax revenues display much greater volatility than the corporate tax base (taxable profits). For the UK for example, large fluctuations in annual corporate profit growth tend to be associated with even larger fluctuations in revenues, and *vice versa*. For the US, Cooper and Knittel (2006, p. 651) find that 'many tax losses are used with a substantial delay' so that 'certain firms and industries suffer a significant penalty from the partial loss refund regime due to the erosion in the real value of their loss refund'. As a result up to 50 per cent of corporate losses remain unused after 10 years, and around 25–30 per cent of losses are never used. This evidence is consistent with the findings of Altshuler and Auerbach (1990) and Auerbach (2007) that cyclical fluctuations in US corporate effective average tax rates are substatially due to tax loss asymmetries.[10] In addition, examining the drivers of tax revenues in OECD countries, Clausing (2007) finds that cyclical changes in those economies' economic growth rates have disproportionately large impacts on their corporate tax revenues; that is, faster growth is associated with a rise in the corporate tax to GDP ratio.

This evidence clearly supports the view that asymmetric tax

---

[10] For the European Union, Agúndez (2006) argues that adopting a common consolidated tax base across EU countries would improve efficiency largely by allowing cross-border tax loss offsets in calculating the common corporate tax base. This might also be expected to have an impact on revenue fluctuations within EU countries.

treatment of losses has a substantial impact on observed revenues over time. This may or may not reflect behavioural responses since, even in the absense of such responses, cyclical fluctuations in revenues and effective tax rates would be expected. However, the evidence in this chapter suggests an additional reason why such cyclical patterns may be expected; namely because behavioural responses are likely to be affected by these asymmetries, generating further cyclical movements in revenues. As mentioned earlier, from the condition in (4.15), behavioural responses may either enhance or mitigate other sources of revenue fluctuations, depending on whether net taxable profit responses to changes in corporate tax rates generate lower or higher tax liabilities compared to when there is no response.

4.4   Conclusions

This chapter has examined the composition of behavioural responses by companies to changes in the taxation of their profits in the home country, and the possible pattern of such responses over the business cycle. Emphasis has been on the determinants of the elasticity of corporation tax paid, by individual firms and in aggregate, in response to a change in the corporation tax rate. This elasticity is closely related to the elasticity of net or taxable profits with respect to a change in the tax rate. In this respect the present analysis may be seen as following the broad agenda set by Feldstein (1995) who emphasised the importance of the elasticity of taxable income with respect to the retention, or net-of-tax, rate.

Firms' responses to tax rate changes can take the form of real responses, in which real activities change or are relocated to other tax jurisdictions, and income-shifting responses in which the location of economic activity is unchanged but the extent to which incomes are declared in the home country changes. This chapter has shown that it is also important to distinguish separate responses of gross profits and of deductions allowable as profit offsets. In particular, the overall elasticity of taxable profits with respect to the tax rate can be decomposed into four elasticities relating to real/shifting and profit/deduction responses, along with the ratio of gross declared profits to taxable profits. The size and type of qualifying expenditures was shown to be important as this determines both the extent of deductions and their endogenous or automatic adjustment in association with profit changes. This endogenous response directly impacts on measures of overall tax responsiveness.

The endogenous deductions response can be summarised by the elasticity of aggregate taxable profits with respect to gross declared profits. This was shown to be pro-cyclical, leading to a variation in the elasticity of total revenue with respect to the tax rate that, *ceteris paribus*, is counter-cyclical. However, this variation is unlikely to be symmetric, being especially pronounced in periods of recession. This asymmetry between booms and recessions arises because of the asymmetric treatment of losses in the tax code, together with the fact that losses tend to be relatively unimportant as tax deductions in circumstances of trend, or above-trend, growth. The asymmetry increases as the amplitude of the profit cycle increases.

An implication of these findings for empirical attempts to measure behavioural responses of tax revenue or profits to corporate tax rate changes, is that the nature and extent of corporate tax deductions, especially losses, can be expected to give rise to quite different behavioural response estimates. This is especially true for countries where tax codes display greater asymmetry in their treatment of losses, and in relatively high loss recession circumstances. In this context, firms are likely to be more constrained by the endogenous tying of deductions to profits claimed in their home jurisdiction. By contrast, even with asymmetric loss treatment, behavioural response estimates may be relatively unaffected when firms' profits are on or above the trend. Existing empirical estimates of corporate behavioural responses differ quite widely even for the same or similar countries. Various conceptual, methodological or practical reasons might account for this. The present chapter suggests that additional factors to consider, largely ignored thus far, are the differential asymmetric treatment of losses across countries, and the point in a country's economic cycle when behavioural responses are estimated.

Part III

A Simulation Model

Chapter 5

The Distribution of Profits

This chapter investigates the form of the distribution of corporate profits in the UK. The static distribution of annual profits is examined along with the dynamics of change from one year to the next. The model of profits presented here is statistical in nature, just as most models of income distribution are statistical, rather than providing an economic model capable of generating a profit distribution, and its changes, resulting from a complex set of economic factors. The motivation is to construct a model of profits, and their dynamics, which may be used as a component in the microsimulation model CorpSim. This model is used in Part IV of this book.

Little information about profits has previously been available to researchers, so that there are few studies of profit distributions and those often concentrate on a single industry: this contrasts with the personal distribution of income which has been subject to extensive empirical analysis. Here gross profits are those defined for tax purposes and are the total profits declared to HMRC as potentially liable for corporation tax. This is distinct from the accounting definition of gross profits where some items of income or expenditure in company accounts are treated differently – for example, interest payments and capital expenditure.

Given the complexity of corporate structures and revenue sources, combined with the paucity of data relating to the distribution of profits in the UK, the approach taken is to construct a simplified model that nevertheless captures the essential characteristics of the changing profit distribution. Consistent with the aim of producing a model which can, as mentioned above, be used as one component in a larger model involving profits, it is necessary to provide more than a descriptive statistical model in terms of the distribution of profits and their changes over time. It is required to construct a model which is capable of simulating profits over a specified time period, including for example a hypothetical business cycle, starting from an initial distribution.

A complicating feature of profits is that most corporations obtain profits from more than one source. It would not be appropriate to consider only one source or simply the aggregate profit over all sources. This is because of the complexity of the corporation tax structure. However, emphasis is placed here on just two sources two correlated profit sources – trading profits and loan-relationship profits which together comprise the main sources. The latest data, for 2003–04, show that in aggregate across financial and non-financial sectors (excluding North Sea Oil and Life Assurance) gross trading profits account for around 77 per cent of total UK-source gross profits with loan-relationship income accounting for a further 16 per cent. When foreign-source income is included the former two profit sources account for around 75 per cent of total gross profit.

Only domestic sources of profit are considered, so that complications arising from international transactions are ignored.

This is not meant to imply that international aspects are unimportant, simply that they cannot easily be incorporated into the present analysis. A further complication, unlike the personal income distribution, is that profits from different sources, and indeed for all sources combined, can be negative. In order to use functional forms which require the variable of interest to be positive, it is necessary to transform profits by 'shifting the axis' an appropriate amount. The model is nevertheless capable of describing the extent to which firms are likely to move between negative and positive profits over time, particularly over the business cycle. The nature of movements between negative and positive values is important when considering the relationship between gross and taxable (or net) profits. This is because of the existence of regulations allowing the use of losses from one source or firm to offset profits from another source or firm within a group (defined for tax purposes), as well as allowing losses to be carried forward to future periods when they may be used to offset positive profits from the same source and firm.

Section 5.1 begins by presenting summary information about the distribution of profits, from two correlated sources, in the UK. Section 5.2 then shows how the distribution for each source can be approximated using a mixture distribution (rather than a single functional form) in order to capture the considerable degree of peakedness and fatness of the tails of profit distributions. Section 5.3 shows how the initial joint distribution of profits from two sources can be generated. Section 5.4 presents the dynamic component of the model describing the changing distribution of profits over time. It describes a simulation model designed to produce profits for a sample of corporations over the business cycle.

5.1 The Form of the Distribution

This section provides a basic description of the form of the distribution of profits. First, Figure 5.1 shows the distribution of trading profits, P^A, for 2003–04, the latest year available. This distribution is based on data for around 160k firms in the HMRC CT600 database: the histogram was obtained using a representative sample of 15k firms.[1] Data on trading profits and losses (Gross Case 1 profits and losses) have been combined to produce the distribution shown. A similar distribution was obtained for loan-relationship profits, P^B, (Gross Case 3 income and losses). This is similar to that shown in Figure 5.1 but is even more concentrated around $-£50$k to $+£50$k, with a mode in the $-£50$k to £0 class. While the distribution in Figure 5.1 is positively skewed, there is clearly a substantial left-hand tail in the region of negative profits. The distribution is highly peaked, as well as containing long flat tails.

To avoid the problems of dealing with negative values, the approach adopted here is first to convert profits into a positive variable, x_t, where:

$$x_t = P_t + d_t \tag{5.1}$$

A choice must therefore be made regarding the shift parameter, d_t, where the same value is applied to both profit sources in each period. Table 5.1 reports values of the mean and variance of logarithms of $P_t + d_t$ for the two sources, designated A and B, for three years, using a range of values for d_t. The table also shows, under the columns for source A, the correlation coeffi-

---

[1] Companies for which this database recorded zero profits and zero turnover were omitted. The CT600 data are derived from information completed by companies on their CT600 form, prior to any assessment or analysis by HMRC. It may therefore include errors which subsequent enquiries correct.

Table 5.1: Summary Measures of Distributions of $P_t + d_t$

	Source A			Source B		
Year	2001–2	2002–3	2003–4	2001–2	2002–3	2003–4
$n = 26088$	$d = 400$					
Mean	6.362	6.364	6.361	6.031	6.029	6.03
Variance	0.712	0.738	0.752	0.047	0.049	0.049
Correlation	0.380	0.376	0.387			
$n = 26500$	$d = 500$					
Mean	6.534	6.538	6.537	6.249	6.248	6.247
Variance	0.623	0.643	0.651	0.045	0.043	0.042
Correlation	0.328	0.350	0.357			
$n = 26847$	$d = 600$					
Mean	6.678	6.682	6.684	6.426	6.425	6.424
Variance	0.559	0.575	0.575	0.042	0.042	0.042
Correlation	0.319	0.335	0.337			
$n = 27142$	$d = 700$					
Mean	6.800	6.809	6.809	6.577	6.576	6.575
Variance	0.519	0.512	0.525	0.032	0.032	0.033
Correlation	0.316	0.335	0.329			
$n = 27402$	$d = 800$					
Mean	6.911	6.920	6.920	6.709	6.708	6.707
Variance	0.470	0.469	0.473	0.010	0.009	0.012
Correlation	0.393	0.444	0.389			
$n = 27633$	$d = 900$					
Mean	7.008	7.018	7.017	6.822	6.822	6.821
Variance	0.446	0.433	0.443	0.030	0.029	0.028
Correlation	0.342	0.349	0.356			
$n = 27811$	$d = 1000$					
Mean	7.099	7.108	7.107	6.926	6.925	6.925
Variance	0.402	0.401	0.412	0.035	0.036	0.037
Correlation	0.315	0.324	0.315			

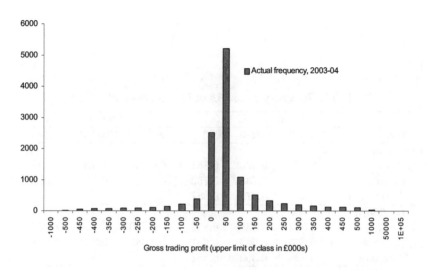

Figure 5.1: The Distribution of Trading Profits: 2003–04

cient between $\log\left(P_t + d_t\right)$ for the two profit sources. Clearly
the sample size is larger as d_t is increased, since more negative
profit values can be included (values are simply truncated below d_t). The variance necessarily falls as the constant term d_t
is increased, while the mean increases. The arithmetic mean of
logarithms of $P_t + d_t$ is higher for trading profits, source A, than
for loan-relationship profits, source B, in all cases. The variance of $\log\left(P_t + d_t\right)$ is substantially higher for source A than for
source B in each period. The values are quite stable over the
three year period.

5.2   A Mixture Distribution

In view of the form of the distribution displayed in Figure 5.1,
a functional form such as the lognormal distribution, which is

widely used in analyses of incomes, is unable to capture the shape of the distribution of P^A+d. The lognormal is defined only for positive values, so that P^A+d is the relevant variable, rather than P^A. The approach taken here is thus to use a mixture distribution, defined as follows.

In general, a mixture distribution, $M(x)$, is defined on the random variable, x, as a linear combination of H independent distributions, $f_i(x)$, such that:

$$M(x) = \sum_{i=1}^{H} \alpha_i f_i(x) \tag{5.2}$$

where α_i defines the proportion of density mass associated with the ith distribution. The use of a mixture distribution, in contrast to the search for a much more complex functional form of a single distribution that can handle the observed characteristics, has several advantages. First, relatively simple distributions can be combined intuitively in order to match particular features of an empirical distribution. Second, relatively straightforward analytical results can be derived for summary measures, despite the overall complexity of the form of the mixture, where well-established analytical results exist for the constituent distributions. For example, the mean and variance associated with the distribution in (5.2) are:

$$E\left[M(x)\right] = \sum_{i=1}^{H} \alpha_i E\left[f_i(x)\right] \tag{5.3}$$

$$V\left[M(x)\right] = \sum_{i=1}^{H} \alpha_i V\left[f_i(x)\right] \tag{5.4}$$

which can by evaluated using the means and variances of the constituent distributions. On the use of (conditional) mixture distributions to handle observed bimodality of the personal income distribution, and changes over time, see Bakker and Creedy (1999).

The following specification, involving a mixture of four distributions, is adopted here for trading profits. A proportion α_1 of the density of $P^A + d$ is modelled using a lognormal distribution $\Lambda\left(\mu_1, \sigma_1^2\right)$, in which σ_1^2 is relatively large to capture a platykurtic or flat feature. This has relatively low kurtosis and thus captures the more central portion of the distribution. To capture the leptokurtic, or peaked, feature, a proportion α_2 is modelled using a lognormal distribution $\Lambda\left(\mu_2, \sigma_2^2\right)$ in which σ_2^2 is relatively small. In the following analysis, $\mu_1 = \mu_2$. However, the use of just these two distributions does not capture the very long tails of the distribution. Hence a further two component distributions are used. The first forms a proportion, α_3, of the density and consists of the upper tail of yet another lognormal distribution, $\Lambda\left(P^A + d > \xi \,\middle|\, \mu_3, \sigma_3^2\right)$, where μ_3 and σ_3^2 are both relatively large. Hence this applies only to values of $P^A + d$ above the threshold, ξ. The importance of this third distribution lies in the fact that the upper tail of the profit distribution is responsible for the bulk of corporation tax payments. For example, when companies are ranked by the size of their corporation tax liabilities in 2003–04, HMRC data show that the largest 8 per cent of all corporation tax payers accounted for almost 90 per cent of all companies' corporation tax liabilities. These same high profit firms are then matched (in groups for tax purposes) with large loss making firms, where values are obtained from the left-hand tail of another lognormal distribution where a much higher value of d is used.

Analysis of the distribution of loan-relationship profits reveals that it does not have the long right tail of the distribution of trading (source A) profits. Hence a mixture distribution involving just two lognormal distributions is used, with proportions of the densities set at α_1 and $\alpha_2 + \alpha_3$ for the platykurtic and leptokurtic components respectively.

5.3   Simulating the Joint Distribution of P^A and P^B

The discussion in the previous section concerned each of the two profit sources in isolation; that is, it concentrated on the marginal distributions of their joint distribution. The summary information in Table 5.1 showed that it is necessary to allow for a positive correlation between these sources. This section shows how the joint distribution of the initial values of $x_A = P^A + d^A$ and $x_B = P^B + d^B$ can be obtained for use in a simulation model of profits.

The approach is to obtain random draws from the appropriate distributional component of x_A, and then to select random draws from the conditional distribution of x_B, given x_A. For each of the major two components of the mixture distribution described in the previous section (that is, excluding the component containing a long upper tail in the case of source A profits), suppose that they are jointly lognormally distributed as:

$$\Lambda\left(x_A, x_B \,|\, \mu_A, \mu_B, \sigma_A^2, \sigma_B^2, \rho\right) \qquad (5.5)$$

In each component of the mixture, the correlation coefficient, ρ, is assumed to be the same.

Consider the ith firm. If v_i^A is a random draw from an $N\left(0, 1\right)$ distribution, an initial value of x_A, obtained from the marginal distribution of x_A, is given by:

$$\log(x_{A,i}) = \mu_A + \sigma_A v_i^A \qquad (5.6)$$

If v_i^B is another random draw from an $N(0,1)$ distribution, an initial value of x_B is obtained from the conditional distribution of x_B, given x_A. Using the fact that $\log(x_B|x_A)$ is normally distributed with mean $\mu_B + \rho \left(\frac{\sigma_A}{\sigma_B}\right)(x_A - \mu_A)$ and variance $\sigma_B^2(1 - \rho^2)$, a simulated value of $x_{B,i}$ is given by:

$$\log(x_{B,i}) = \mu_B + \rho\left(\frac{\sigma_A}{\sigma_B}\right)(x_{A,i} - \mu_A) + \left\{\sigma_B\sqrt{1-\rho^2}\right\}v_i^B \quad (5.7)$$

Hence:

$$P_i^A = x_{A,i} - d^A \qquad (5.8)$$

and:

$$P_i^B = x_{B,i} - d^B \qquad (5.9)$$

In the case of the component capturing the long upper tail of the distribution of source A profits, all random draws from x_A which are less than ξ are rejected.

In generating the distribution of source B profits, the upper tail component is not used and, instead, additional density (the proportion α_3) is added to the peaked component of the distribution. This is because, as mentioned above, the histograms of loan-relationship profits do not display such a long upper tail, but are even more peaked than those of source A profits.

5.3.1 Calibrating the Model

In view of the special nature of the model described above, the approach taken here is to 'calibrate' the model by selecting parameter values which, in combination, produce profit distributions for both sources which are reasonable approximations to the actual distributions. The objective here is not to mimic the distribution in Figure 5.1 precisely, but to capture its essential characteristics so that the simulated distribution approximates, for example, the extent of losses and the distribution of profit levels relative to tax thresholds.

Table 5.2 shows a suitable set of parameter values for the profit distributions. First, it is necessary to specify the maximum initial losses, d^A and d^B, which allows the means and variances of the three lognormal profit distributions in the initial period (separately for $x_{A,i}$ and $x_{B,i}$) to be set. Then the proportions of the density contributed by each of the components of the mixture distributions need to be specified. The correlations between profit sources are then required.

Table 5.2: Parameters of the Profit Distributions

Parameter value		Description
6.425	0.35	Mean and variance of log(profit+d): A
6.425	0.05	Mean and variance of log(profit+d): B
600k		Maximum -ve profit: A and B
0.05		Correlation between profit sources
0.45		Proportion peaked component
6.425	0.001	Mean and variance of log(profit+d): peaked A
6.425	0.0001	Mean and variance of log(profit+d): peaked B
0.10		Proportion in upper tail: A
8.5	1.8	Mean and variance of log(profit+d): A upper tail
1500k		Profit threshold for upper tail: A

Specifying d^A and d^B using the minimum values observed in the CT600 dataset is not appropriate, since these are extremely large values – in the hundred millions or billions. When added to the P_i values, they would generate distributions of x_i that cannot approximate the characteristics observed in Figure 5.1. Experimentation suggested that setting $d^A = d^B = £600$k, to-

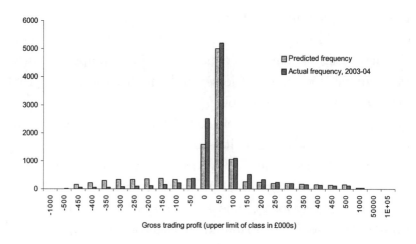

Figure 5.2: Actual and Simulated Trading Profits, 2003-04

gether with the means and variances similar to those shown in
Table 5.1, yielded reasonably close approximations for the P^A
and P^B distributions. For example, the resulting distribution of
P^A (trading profits) is shown in Figure 5.2. This captures the
peakedness of the distribution fairly well, but with numbers in
the larger loss classes slightly over-predicted. The means of logarithms in Table 5.2 are somewhat less than corresponding values
shown in Table 5.1. This is because the distribution shown in
Figure 5.2 is actually that obtained after allowing the simulation
model to run for ten years. Hence some assumed trend growth
operates; the dynamics are discussed in the following section.

As Table 5.2 shows, the initial distribution is modelled using
platykurtic and leptokurtic lognormal distributions, for both A
and B, with the same means (6.425), but with the former having
a larger variance (0.35 versus 0.05 for A; 0.001 versus 0.0001 for
B). For profit source A, the third distribution, contributing only

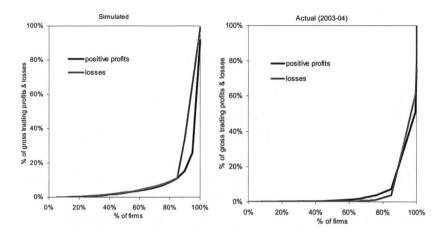

Figure 5.3: Simulated and Empirical Lorenz Curves for Profits and Losses

to the 10 per cent of firms in the upper tail, has a much higher mean and variance (8.5 and 1.8 respectively). Furthermore, values of $x_i < 1500k$ generated from this distribution component are ignored. Table 5.2 also shows a correlation between A and B profits of $\rho = 0.05$; see equation (5.5).

The ability of CorpSim to match actual data on firms' profits and losses can be seen in Figure 5.3. This shows Lorenz curves for observed (positive) trading profits and losses, for the year 2003–04, and those obtained by simulation. It can be seen that the actual distributions of both profits and losses are highly unequal, and this feature is well captured by the simulated equivalents, with the latter displaying slightly less concentration. As a further check, the aggregate ratio of all deductions to gross declared profits, D/P^*, can be compared with actual data from HMRC. The most recent (2002–03 and 2003–04) observed ratios are 0.56 and 0.53; equivalent values produced by CorpSim are around 0.52.

5.4   The Dynamics of Profits

This section describes the specification of the dynamics of gross profits. The dynamic component contains both systematic and stochastic elements, and is designed to generate changes in the distribution of profits over time by tracing the profits of each of a large number of firms over a required time period. The model does not allow for 'births' and 'deaths' of firms, or shifts into or out of the tax jurisdiction, but considers a fixed population over a given time period.

5.4.1   Dynamics for a Single Profit Source

Given, as before, $x_t = P_t + d_t$, the basic assumption is that x_t is subject to a growth rate made up of a systematic component, g_t, and a random component, u_t. However, experiments showed that including regression towards the mean quickly 'squeezed' the two long tails of the distributions of A and B profits, producing too much density in the middle ranges, so that the peakedness of the distribution was also much reduced. The t subscript on g allows the systematic growth of profits to vary in some way over time, along with the minimum profit. Thus x is specified to change according to:

$$x_t = x_{t-1}\left(1 + g_t + u_t\right) \tag{5.10}$$

Furthermore, serial correlation implies that:

$$u_t = \gamma u_{t-1} + v_t \tag{5.11}$$

and v is assumed to be Normally distributed as $N\left(0, \sigma_v^2\right)$. In terms of P_t, (5.10) becomes:

$$P_t + d_t = (P_{t-1} + d_{t-1})(1 + g_t + u_t) \qquad (5.12)$$

and rearrangement gives:

$$P_t = P_{t-1}(1 + g_t + u_t) - (d_t - d_{t-1}) + d_{t-1}(g_t + u_t) \qquad (5.13)$$

This is the basic equation describing the systematic (g_t, d_t) and stochastic (u_t) processes generating the changing profit level of each firm, and hence the changing distribution of profits over time. It is completed by the specification of the time profiles of g_t and d_t.

The time profiles of g_t and d_t could be specified in a number of ways. For example, historical or forecast data could be used to specify annual growth rates. However, suppose that the growth rate, g_t, is composed of a constant component, g^*, representing inflation and/or trend real growth, and a real cyclical component, g_t^c. This cyclical aspect can be described by an amplitude of a_g and a wavelength of w_g. Using a sine wave to represent the cycle, then:

$$
\begin{aligned}
g_t &= g^* + g_t^c \\
&= g^* + a_g \sin\left(\frac{2\pi t}{w_g}\right) \qquad (5.14)
\end{aligned}
$$

Similarly, suppose that the proportional rate of change in d (the maximum loss) from one period to the next consists of a fixed term, $\dot{d}^*$, and a cyclical component, $\dot{d}_t^c$. Thus:

$$d_t = d_{t-1}\left(1 + \dot{d}^* + \dot{d}_t^c\right) \qquad (5.15)$$

The cyclical component similarly has an amplitude of a_d and a wavelength of w_d, so that:

$$d_t = d_{t-1}\left(1 + \dot{d}^* + a_d \sin\left(\frac{2\pi t}{w_d}\right)\right) \qquad (5.16)$$

This captures the notion that the extent of maximum losses can also behave cyclically; for example, in a recession when profit growth is lower on average, maximum losses are likely to become larger.

5.4.2 Two Profit Sources

This subsection extends the above model to the case where firms obtain profits from two sources, A and B. These two income sources give rise to profits of P^A and P^B, with corresponding values of $x_A = P^A + d^A$ and $x_B = P^B + d^B$. Starting from a given initial joint distribution of profits, such that there is some correlation, ρ, between A and B profits, it is necessary to generate profit flows in subsequent periods. The following sequence is used.

First, the random component of proportional changes for the A source is given, where $v_{u,i}^A$ is a random draw from an $N(0,1)$ distribution, by:

$$u_{i,t}^A = \gamma u_{i,t-1}^A + \sigma_{u_A} v_{u,i}^A \qquad (5.17)$$

To allow for the possibility that stochastic shocks to A and B may be correlated, assume that u^A and u^B are jointly Normally distributed as

$$N\left(u^A, u^B \,\middle|\, 0, 0, \sigma_{u_A}, \sigma_{u_B}, \rho\right). \qquad (5.18)$$

A value of u^B is then given by:

$$u_{i,t}^B = \rho\left(\frac{\sigma_{u_A}}{\sigma_{u_B}}\right) u_{i,t}^A + \left\{\sigma_{u_B}\sqrt{1-\rho^2}\right\} v_{u,i}^B \qquad (5.19)$$

Thus, the two profit sources are generated using:

$$P_{i,t}^A = P_{i,t-1}^A \left(1 + g_t^A + u_{i,t}^A\right) - \left(d_t^A - d_{t-1}^A\right) + d_{t-1}^A \left(g_t^A + u_{i,t}^A\right)$$

(5.20)

and:

$$P_{i,t}^B = P_{i,t-1}^B \left(1 + g_t^B + u_{i,t}^B\right) - \left(d_t^B - d_{t-1}^B\right) + d_{t-1}^B \left(g_t^B + u_{i,t}^B\right)$$

(5.21)

Separate growth cycles, corresponding to (5.14) and (5.16) can then be specified for each of the terms g_t^A, d_t^A, and so on.

5.4.3 Profit Growth Rates

In the above model it is important to recognise that the absence of a stochastic component of proportionate changes in profits does not imply that all profits grow at the same rate. Consider a single profit source where, as above, $P_t = x_t - d_t$, with x and d growing at rates δ and θ respectively. These rates differ because the growth cycles of x and d are expected to be out of phase – in boom periods with relatively high δ it is likely that θ is relatively low. Combining these assumptions gives the result that:

$$\frac{P_t - P_{t-1}}{P_{t-1}} = \delta - \frac{d_{t-1}}{P_{t-1}} (\delta - \theta)$$

(5.22)

For large profit makers the term d_{t-1}/P_{t-1} is low and hence the growth rate of profits is similar at δ. However, for loss-makers, $-1 < d_{t-1}/P_{t-1} < \infty$. For the largest loss makers d_{t-1}/P_{t-1} is close to unity and the growth rate of profits is close to θ.

5.5 Conclusions

This chapter has described a model of the distribution and dynamics of UK corporate profits. The aim was to construct a model that is capable of providing the basis of a corporate tax microsimulation model which can generate profits over a number of years. Although many simplifications were required in constructing and calibrating the model, it is able to capture many of the crucial features of the distribution of profits in the UK and their relative movements.

Chapter 6

Modelling Deductions

A crucial component of CorpSim consists of a mechanism for determining the way in which firms use their losses and capital allowances to transform their total gross profit (that is, profits from both income sources) into taxable, or net, profit. Given taxable profit for each firm, it is then a simple matter to apply the UK corporation tax structure. The situation facing a single firm is examined in section 6.1, and is obviously much simpler than that facing firms within a group. The case of groups consisting of two firms is examined in section 6.2.

6.1 Single Firms

This section describes the way in which the total net profit, that is profit after all deductions, of a single firm is calculated in CorpSim. Consider a firm which, as above, receives profit from two sources A and B in period t of P_t^A and P_t^B respectively. Total gross profit, P_t, is thus:

$$P_t = P_t^A + P_t^B \qquad (6.1)$$

It is necessary to transform total gross profit into total net profit by subtracting any capital allowances and losses. In practice, the use of such deductions by a firm may depend on its expectations regarding future profits and losses arising from the two sources. However, without a clear view of, and indeed information about, the main determinants of expected future profits, the present model abstracts from the consideration of profit expectations. The use of capital allowances is described in subsection 6.1.1 and the use of losses is examined in subsection 6.1.2. The way in which priorities in making deductions are modelled is then described in subsection 6.1.3. An illustrative example is provided in Section 6.1.4.

6.1.1   Capital Allowances

Capital allowances are calculated using fiscal depreciation rules applied to firms' investment expenditures, which requires these expenditures to be specified. The capital allowances generated from investment are assumed to arise entirely in association with the firm's trade and hence are deductible from trading profits. This reflects the vast majority of investment expenditure for which firms claim capital allowances in practice. However, the level of investment expenditure undertaken by firms may be determined by a number of variables, among which the firm's various sources of profits are likely to be important. Capital allowances are used to offset A profits, and any 'excess' capital allowances may be used to offset B profits.

Let I_t denote investment in period t. The model assumes that investment is a simple function of both A and B profits such that:

$$I_t = \alpha + \beta \left[\theta \left(P_t^A + \phi P_t^B \right) + (1 - \theta) \left(P_{t-1}^A + \phi P_{t-1}^B \right) \right] \quad (6.2)$$

Hence, investment is a linear function of the weighted average of the current and previous period's weighted sum of profits from the two sources. These weights can be specified to reflect alternative views regarding the relative importance of different profit sources or time horizons in the determination of investment. With $\beta, \phi > 0$, the specification in (6.2) allows for investment to be positively related to either or both types of profit and for a limited lagged response. If $\phi = 0$, only trading profits determine investment, and $\theta = 1$ implies only current profits are relevant, while $\theta = 0$ implies that only lagged profits affect investment.

Capital allowances depend on investment by the firm and the fiscal depreciation regime. In the UK, the fiscal depreciation rules for plant and machinery investment, and investment in industrial buildings, are different. The former are depreciated on a writing-down basis at a rate of 25 per cent per year, while the latter are depreciated on a straight-line basis over 25 years. However, plant and machinery investment dominates capital allowances empirically and, for this reason, only this is modelled below.

With investment in period t of I_t, capital allowances available in period t are denoted, CA_t^A. The A superscript in this terms reflects the fact that capital allowances relate to A-source profits. Where $\delta = 0.25$ is the depreciation rate, allowances are given by:

$$
\begin{aligned}
CA_t^A &= \delta I_t + \delta(1-\delta)I_{t-1} + \delta(1-\delta)^2 I_{t-2} + \dots \\
&= \delta \left(I_t + CP_{t-1}^A \right)
\end{aligned} \tag{6.3}
$$

where $CP_{t-1}^A = \delta(1-\delta)I_{t-1} + \delta(1-\delta)^2 I_{t-2} + \dots$ is the pool of capital allowances available at period t, arising from previous periods' investments. The present analysis abstracts from the phenomenon of capital allowance 'disclaiming' in which some firms postpone claims for capital allowances, such that $\delta_i <$ 0.25. If there are insufficient A profits against which to claim capital allowances, 'excess' capital allowances, XCA_t, are said to arise. These may be deducted from B profits. Alternatively they may be used to generate a trading loss, such that $P_t^A - CA_t^A < 0$, which is then added to the A loss pool, LP_t^A, to be carried forward to the next period. How firms choose between these alternatives is specified below. The capital allowance pool available at the end of period t, to be carried forward, is given by:

$$CP_t^A = (1 - \delta)\left\{CP_{t-1}^A + I_t\right\} \tag{6.4}$$

6.1.2 The Use of Losses

If a firm makes a loss in period t, such that $L_t^A = -P_t^A > 0$ or $L_t^B = -P_t^B > 0$, these may be claimed concurrently against P_t^B or P_t^A. Alternatively, they may be carried forward and claimed against future profits of the same source. As a result, in any given period, t, there may be loss pools from the previous period, denoted LP_{t-1}^A and LP_{t-1}^B, which are available to offset current A and B profits respectively.

The corporation tax rules used for modelling loss use are shown in Table 6.1. These are the rules governing trading and loan-relationship losses used in practice, with the exception that carrying back of losses is omitted from the model.

6.1.3 Priorities in Claiming Deductions

The order in which deductions are claimed against gross profits is determined in part by the corporation tax rules and in part by firms' choices. In the simplified model here, where there are only

Table 6.1: Corporation Tax Rules and the Use of Losses

Profit	Used in-year against:		Group-	Carried forward:	
source	same	other	relieved	within	across
	source	source	in-year	source	source
A: Trading	Yes	Yes	Yes	Yes	No
B: Loan-relationship	Yes	Yes	Yes	Yes	No

two profit sources, capital allowances are first deducted from *A* profits. In the absence of disclaiming, this order is dictated by the tax code. Whether any excess capital allowances should be carried forward as an *A* loss, or used currently against *B* profits is a choice allowable under the tax code. The size and type of losses brought forward from previous periods may also be relevant to this decision. Clearly, the use of excess allowances to offset *B* profits is more likely if expectations of future *A* profits are low and current *B* profits are high. In the absence of any information on profit expectations, the current model assumes that all firms prefer to offset any current losses or excess capital allowances against any currently available profits, rather than carry them forward to future periods when they can no longer be used across profit sources. This reflects a view that the expected net present value of current losses and capital allowances as profit offsets is greater in the current period. If a firm faces a choice, its ability to claim deductions, and the order in which they are claimed, depend on the size and source of its profits.

Table 6.2 shows the assumed order, moving down the table, in which deductions are claimed for the four possible combinations of profits and losses for *A* and *B* for a single firm *i*. This table shows that, in general, the order in which deductions are claimed

Table 6.2: Profit Combinations for a Single Firm

Profit combination	Profit source	
	A	B
$P_i^A > 0; P_i^B > 0$	CA_t	
	LA_{t-1}	XCA_t
		LB_{t-1}
$P_i^A > 0; P_i^B < 0$	CA_t	
	LB_t	
	LA_{t-1}	
$P_i^A < 0; P_i^B > 0$		XCA_t
		LA_t
		LB_{t-1}
$P_i^A < 0; P_i^B < 0$	–	–

is as follows. First, capital allowances are claimed against A profits, with any excess capital allowances then claimed against B. Second, current A or B losses (LA_t, LB_t) are claimed against current profits across sources. Third, past losses are brought forward and used within source.

6.1.4   An Illustrative Example

Table 6.3 provides an example of how net profits are calculated in CorpSim where only single firms are considered. This shows two firms, i and j, where the former makes positive A and B profits in year t, while the latter makes an A loss of £800. The two firms also have loss pools brought forward from previous periods as shown in square brackets below line 1, and capital allowances given in line 2. The method for calculating net profits first deducts capital allowances from A profits, where possible.

For firm j the A loss means that excess capital allowances are carried across and deducted from B profits of £150, yielding line 3. As line 4 shows, £100 of current losses are then deducted

Table 6.3: Illustrative Net Profit Calculation: Single Firms

Profits:	Firm i		Firm j	
	A: Trading	B: Non-trading	A: Trading	B: Non-trading
1. Gross Profit	1100	500	**-800**	150
[Loss pool:LP_{t-1}]	[5000]	[200]	[100]	[100]
2. Less Cap. Allow	-100		-50	
3. = 1. minus 2.	1000	500	-800	100
4. Less L_t	-	-	-	**-100**
5. Less LP_{t-1}	-1000	-200	-	0
6. **Net Profit**	0	**300**	0	0
7. [Loss Pool:LP_t]	[4000]	[0]	[800]	[100]

from j's B profits (after capital allowances) to yield zero net B profits, shown in line 6. The remaining £700 of current A losses are added to the £100 A loss pool from previous periods to give a current A loss pool of £800, as in line 7. Past B losses of £100 are also carried forward, in line 7. For firm i, having no current losses, past losses can immediately be deducted from profits, after capital allowances, to yield net A profits of zero and net B profits of £300 (line 6). Remaining losses in the loss pool are carried forward (line 7).

6.2 Firms in Groups

This section describes the procedure used in CorpSim where firms join to form groups, but individual firms continue to be taxed on an unconsolidated basis. The UK corporation tax system permits firms' losses and excess capital allowances to be used as deductions against the profits of group members with positive gross profits. This takes the form of group relief, which is surrendered by group loss-makers to partners in profit. The corporate tax base is composed of many single firms and also many multi-firm groups, where there can be as many as hundreds of firms in one group. Modelling the group relief associated with this complex type of multi-firm group is beyond the scope of the present model.

Firms are assumed to form groups consisting of pairs of firms. Although having only two members of a group may seem restrictive, the key analytical aspect of group relief for present purposes is that members of a group with losses can surrender (all or some of) those losses to members with positive profits. The two group members represented in the model can therefore be thought of as capturing the sum of loss-making group members in practice and similarly for profit-makers. This method therefore captures the essential characteristic of group relief, whereby losses can only be carried across firms contemporaneously. To simplify the analysis, group relief of excess capital allowances is not considered. The priorities in claiming group deductions are discussed in subsection 6.2.1 and examples for two hypothetical firms in a group are provided in subsection 6.2.2.

6.2.1   Priorities in Claiming Group Deductions

Modelling firms' priorities in claiming deductions within groups is substantially complicated by the number of profit and loss combinations, even with only two profit sources and two firms in a group. In this simple case there are nevertheless 16 possible arrangements of profits and losses associated with A and B profit sources. These are shown in Table 6.4. With only one firm, Table 6.2 showed 4 combinations, equivalent to rows 1, 5, 9, and 13 in Table 6.4. With an additional firm, for each of these first 4 combinations, there are a further 4 combinations for the second firm. However, the following rows are equivalent if i and j are reversed: $2 = 5$; $3 = 9$; $4 = 13$; $10 = 7$; $8 = 14$; $12 = 15$. Hence 10 different cases need to be considered.

Table 6.4: Profit Combinations: Two Firms

Combination	P_i^A	P_i^B	P_j^A	P_j^B
1	> 0	> 0	> 0	> 0
2	> 0	> 0	> 0	< 0
3	> 0	> 0	< 0	> 0
4	> 0	> 0	< 0	< 0
5	> 0	< 0	> 0	> 0
6	> 0	< 0	> 0	< 0
7	> 0	< 0	< 0	> 0
8	> 0	< 0	< 0	< 0
9	< 0	> 0	> 0	> 0
10	< 0	> 0	> 0	< 0
11	< 0	> 0	< 0	> 0
12	< 0	> 0	< 0	< 0
13	< 0	< 0	> 0	> 0
14	< 0	< 0	> 0	< 0
15	< 0	< 0	< 0	> 0
16	< 0	< 0	< 0	< 0

The order in which deductions are assumed to be claimed for the group case is as follows. First, as for single firms, capital allowances are deducted within firms, wherever possible, including excess capital allowances claimed across B profits, where there are insufficient A profits. Since current losses can only be group-relived if surrendered or received concurrently, these are deducted next. However, it might be expected that groups would wish to use both current and past losses in a tax minimising manner. This is likely to be affected by various business factors unrelated to taxation and by the tax consequences of expectations regarding future profits and losses; for example by shifting losses out of companies where they are expected to be stranded for some time. As with single firms, the model abstracts from profit expectations by groups. However, it is still the case that groups are likely to be faced with choices over the use of past and current losses, within and between members, which affect the group's overall tax liability.

The simulation model therefore employs a search procedure which seeks to deduct losses (from profits net of capital allowances) such that both current and past losses are used in ways that minimise current net profits within the group, and any remaining losses to be carried forward. For example, group net profits may be reduced to zero via a number of alternative allocations of losses, but some of these involve greater use of past losses than others (fewer stranded losses). The search procedure used allocates losses within and between firms to ensure that the option with minimum group net profits and least stranded losses is achieved. Minimisation of group net profits does not guarantee tax minimisation, for example, if one small group member is taxed at 19 per cent whilst the other is taxed at 30 per cent. However, with the exception of these rare cases, tax minimisation can generally be presumed from this procedure.

It is possible to specify an alternative approach taking a more mechanical view of the use of deductions. This would involve deductions being subtracted from profits in a fixed order, following a set of rules of thumb, rather than attempting to minimise group net profits. For example, deductions could be subtracted in the following order: capital allowances, current losses deducted within firms, excess capital allowances, group relief, losses brought forward within firms from previous periods. In simulations reported in Part IV, this simpler alternative is compared with the more complex algorithm described above.

6.2.2 Illustrative Examples

Table 6.5 repeats the illustration for single firms in Table 6.3, but for the case where firms i and j are in a group. This configuration of profits corresponds to case 3 in Table 6.4. Gross profits, loss pools and capital allowances in year t are as in the previous example. Capital allowances are again deducted first to give profits, net of capital allowances, shown in line 3.

Table 6.5: Illustrative Net Profit Calculation: Groups

		Firm i		Firm j	
Profits:	A: Trading	B: Non-trading	A: Trading	B: Non-trading
1. Gross Profit	1100	500	-800	150
[Loss pool:LP_{t-1}]	[5000]	[200]	[100]	[100]
2. Less Cap. Allow	-100	-	-50 $\longrightarrow$	
3. = 1. minus 2.	1000	500	-800	100
4. Less L_t	-200	-500	-	100
5. Less LP_{t-1}	-800	0	-	0
6. **Net Profit**	0	0	0	0
7. [Loss Pool:LP_t]	[4200]	[200]	[100]	[100]

The issue for the group is how to allocate the £800 A-loss in firm j to minimise group net profits. These could all be allocated to reduce i's A profits of £1000, in line 3, but because i also has a large A loss pool from previous periods (£5000) this would leave £4800 of these stranded until a future period. If j's losses of £800 are surrendered to offset i's A profits, only £200 of i's previous A losses could be used in year t, to reduce i's net A profits to zero. As line 4 of Table 6.5 shows, by allocating the £800 loss in the way indicated, group net profits become zero, and the minimum possible loss pools (£4600) are carried forward to $t + 1$. In the earlier single firm illustration, total net profits were positive and loss pools totalling £4900 were carried forward to $t+1$. This illustration therefore demonstrates the capacity for group formation to reduce both current tax liabilities and the time lag between the creation of losses and their use as profit offsets. Both of these properties can affect the time-series profile of corporation tax revenues over the economic cycle.

The following examples illustrate how the algorithm to minimise group net profits and stranded losses is applied to the various gross profit and loss combinations which can arise within groups of two firms, labelled i and j. Of the ten possible combinations discussed in the text, there are eight cases where sharing of losses is an option. The other cases are where profits from all sources are positive, or all are negative.

Tables 6.6 to 6.9 show three examples each for the eight combinations of interest. To focus on the use of losses, capital allowances are set to zero in all cases. These examples represent three alternative configurations of current losses and loss pools to be carried forward and used as profit offsets. These examples are:

i. Losses arising within the group in period t are greater than the sum of positive profits (net of capital allowances) within the group in period t. In this case the maximum possible available losses are used to off-set positive profits, and there is no use in period t of loss pools brought forward from period $t - 1$. Unused losses arising in period t are added to the relevant loss pools carried forward to period $t + 1$.

ii. Losses arising within the group in period t are less than the sum of positive profits (net of capital allowances) within the group in period t, and these profits net of current losses exceed the sum of the available loss pools from period $t-1$. In this case, all available current losses are used to offset positive profits in period t, and all loss pools brought forward from period $t-1$ can also be used in period t.

iii. Losses arising within the group in period t are less than the sum of positive profits (net of capital allowances) within the group in period t, but profits net of current losses are less than the sum of the available loss pools from period $t-1$. In this case, all available current losses are used to offset positive profits in period t, and only a fraction of the available loss pools brought forward from period $t-1$ can be used in period t.

Example (iii) therefore requires a search procedure to identify the optimal allocation of current losses and losses brought forward. The optimum in this case is that combination which both minimises group net profits (and hence tax, for a given tax rate), and the carry forward of losses to period $t+1$, where they could become stranded in future. In Tables 6.6 to 6.9 the terms θ_1 and θ_2 indicate the resulting proportions of losses used as group relief to off-set A and B profits respectively (from firm i to firm j or *vice versa*). Tables 6.6 to 6.9 also record the number of cases examined in order to identify the optimal values of θ_1 and θ_2. The remaining proportion, $1 - \theta_1 - \theta_2$, is used within the loss-making firm, if $\theta_1 + \theta_2 < 1$. Having searched across all possible combinations, there may be several values of θ_1 and θ_2 which achieve the optimum outcome. In this case, the simulation model chooses the first one identified.

Table 6.6: Use of Losses: Cases 2 and 3

	Case 2			Case 3		
Example:	(i)	(ii)	(iii)	(i)	(ii)	(iii)
Firm i						
Profit A:	400	400	1000	400	400	1000
Profit B:	200	200	500	200	200	500
Initial LP A	500	50	5000	500	50	5000
Initial LP B	100	100	200	100	100	200
net profit A:	0	100	0	0	0	0
net profit B:	0	0	0	0	100	0
loss claimed A:	0	0	0	0	0	0
loss claimed B:	0	0	0	0	0	0
loss pool A:	500	0	4200	500	0	4200
loss pool B:	100	0	200	100	0	200
Firm j						
Profit A:	100	100	100	-800	-400	-800
Profit B:	-800	-400	-800	100	100	100
Initial LP A	50	50	100	50	100	100
Initial LP B	50	100	100	50	50	100
net profit A:	0	0	0	0	0	0
net profit B:	0	0	0	0	0	0
loss claimed A:	0	0	0	700	400	800
loss claimed B:	700	400	800	0	0	0
loss pool A:	50	0	100	150	100	100
loss pool B:	150	100	100	50	0	100
θ_1:	0	0	0.25	0	0	0.25
θ_2:	0	0	0.625	0	0	0.625
Cases examined:	0	0	147	0	0	147

Table 6.7: Use of Losses: Cases 4 and 6

	Case 4			Case 6		
Example:	(i)	(ii)	(iii)	(i)	(ii)	(iii)
Firm i						
Profit A:	200	1000	1000	200	1200	1200
Profit B:	300	300	300	-300	-300	-300
Initial LP A	100	100	1000	100	100	1000
Initial LP B	200	200	200	200	200	200
net profit A:	0	100	0	0	600	0
net profit B:	0	0	0	0	0	0
loss claimed A:	0	0	0	0	0	0
loss claimed B:	0	0	0	200	300	300
loss pool A:	100	0	607.5	100	0	300
loss pool B:	200	0	192.5	300	200	200
Firm j						
Profit A:	-600	-600	-600	400	400	400
Profit B:	-300	-300	-300	-500	-500	-500
Initial LP A	100	100	100	100	100	100
Initial LP B	200	200	200	200	200	200
net profit A:	0	0	0	0	0	0
net profit B:	0	0	0	0	0	0
loss claimed A:	200	600	600	0	0	0
loss claimed B:	300	300	300	400	500	500
loss pool A:	500	100	100	100	0	0
loss pool B:	200	200	200	300	200	200
θ_1:	0	0	0.675	0	0	0.375
θ_2:	0	0	0	0	0	0
Cases examined:	0	0	14	0	0	21

Table 6.8: Use of Losses: Cases 8 and 10

Example:	Case 8			Case 10		
	(i)	(ii)	(iii)	(i)	(ii)	(iii)
Firm i						
Profit A:	200	1200	1200	-300	-300	-300
Profit B:	-300	-50	-50	300	1300	1300
Initial LP A	100	100	1000	100	100	100
Initial LP B	200	200	200	200	200	1200
net profit A:	0	650	0	0	0	0
net profit B:	0	0	0	0	800	0
loss claimed A:	0	0	0	300	300	300
loss claimed B:	200	50	50	0	0	0
loss pool A:	100	0	250	100	100	100
loss pool B:	300	200	200	200	0	110
Firm j						
Profit A:	-800	-100	-100	600	600	600
Profit B:	-300	-300	-300	-800	-300	-300
Initial LP A	100	100	100	100	100	1000
Initial LP B	200	200	200	200	200	200
net profit A:	0	0	0	5	200	0
net profit B:	0	0	0	0	0	0
loss claimed A:	0	100	100	0	0	0
loss claimed B:	0	300	300	600	300	300
loss pool A:	900	100	100	100	0	790
loss pool B:	500	200	200	400	200	200
θ_1:	0	0	0	0	0	0.65
θ_2:	0	0	0	0	0	0
Cases examined:	0	0	0	21	0	41

Table 6.9: Use of Losses: Cases 11 and 12

	Case 11			Case 12		
Example:	(i)	(ii)	(iii)	(i)	(ii)	(iii)
Firm i						
Profit A:	-200	-200	-200	-200	-200	-200
Profit B:	300	1300	1300	300	1300	1300
Initial LP A	100	100	100	100	100	100
Initial LP B	200	50	800	200	200	800
net profit A:	0	0	0	0	0	0
net profit B:	0	450	0	0	200	0
loss claimed A:	200	200	200	200	200	200
loss claimed B:	0	0	0	0	0	0
loss pool A:	100	100	100	100	100	100
loss pool B:	200	0	225	200	0	400
Firm j						
Profit A:	-800	-800	-800	-400	-400	-400
Profit B:	300	300	300	-300	-300	-300
Initial LP A	100	100	100	100	100	100
Initial LP B	200	100	200	200	200	200
net profit A:	0	0	0	0	0	0
net profit B:	0	0	0	0	0	0
loss claimed A:	400	800	800	0	400	400
loss claimed B:	0	0	0	100	300	300
loss pool A:	500	100	100	500	100	100
loss pool B:	200	0	175	400	200	200
θ_1:	0	0	0.275	0	0	0
θ_2:	0	0	0	0	0	0
Cases examined:	0	0	13	0	0	0

6.2.3 Further Details of Case 2

To illustrate how the model allocates losses, the three examples shown for Case 2 in Table 6.6 are described in more detail here. Table 6.10 shows example (i) where only current losses are used to offset positive profits. Table 6.11 shows example (ii), where both current losses, and all available loss pools, can be used to offset positive profits. Table 6.12 shows example (iii), where all current losses, and a fraction of available loss pools, can be used to offset positive profits.

Case 2 (i) is relatively straightforward. With available profits less than available losses within the group, losses are allocated to the three gross profit sources in positive profit as shown, to reduce net profits (and hence tax liabilities) to zero. Some period t losses are carried forward to $t + 1$.

Case 2 (ii) is also relatively straightforward but all current losses and past losses can be used. All past losses, LP_{t-1}, are deducted. All current losses are also deducted and are allocated in the following order: first against profits within the same firm, second across firms within the same source (A or B), third across firms and profit source. In Case 2 (ii) this means that £250 of losses are deducted from i's A profits, leaving net A profits of £100. All other net profits are reduced to zero.

Case 2 (iii) is more complex because not all past losses can be used as deductions in period t. However Table 6.12 shows that by setting $\theta_1 = 0.25$, and $\theta_2 = 0.625$, this allows all current losses to be used and the maximum past losses of £4600 are also used. Thus, all net profits are zero in period t and the minimum losses are carried forward. To see this, consider the alternative where instead of firm j's B losses being used to reduce firm i's

Table 6.10: Use of Losses: Case 2 (i)

Profits:	Firm i		Firm j	
	A: Trading	B: Non-trading	A: Trading	B: Non-trading
1. Gross Profit	400	200	100	**-800**
[Loss pool:LP_{t-1}]	[500]	[100]	[50]	[50]
2. Less Cap. Allow	0	0	0	0
3. = 1. minus 2.	400	200	100	-800
4. Less L_t	**-400**	**-200**	**-100**	-
5. Less LP_{t-1}	0	0	0	-
6. Net Profit	0	0	0	0
7. [Loss Pool:LP_t]	[500]	[100]	[50]	[150]

Table 6.11: Use of Losses: Case 2 (ii)

Profits:	Firm i		Firm j	
	A: Trading	B: Non-trading	A: Trading	B: Non-trading
1. Gross Profit	400	200	100	**-400**
[Loss pool:LP_{t-1}]	[50]	[100]	[50]	[100]
2. Less Cap. Allow	0	0	0	0
3. = 1. minus 2.	400	200	100	-400
4. Less L_t	**-250**	**-100**	**-50**	-
5. Less LP_{t-1}	-50	-100	-50	-
6. Net Profit	100	0	0	0
7. [Loss Pool:LP_t]	[0]	[0]	[0]	[100]

Table 6.12: Use of Losses: Case 2 (iii)

Profits:	Firm i		Firm j	
	A: Trading	B: Non-trading	A: Trading	B: Non-trading
1. Gross Profit	1000	500	100	**-800**
[Loss pool:LP_{t-1}]	[5000]	[200]	[100]	[100]
2. Less Cap. Allow	0	0	0	0
3. = 1. minus 2.	1000	500	100	-800
4. Less L_t	-200	-500	-100	-
5. Less LP_{t-1}	-800	0	0	-
6. **Net Profit**	0	0	0	0
7. [Loss Pool:LP_t]	[4200]	[200]	[100]	[100]
	$\theta_1 = 0.25$	$\theta_2 = 0.625$	$1 - \theta_1 - \theta_2 = 0.125$	

B profits by £500 and its *A* profits by £200 (as shown), this is reversed. A reworking of the numbers in Table 6.12 readily shows that firm *i*'s net *B* profits, liable to tax, would now be £100 (all others are zero) and losses carried forward would sum to £4700.

6.3 Conclusions

This chapter has described algorithms for determining the use of capital and allowances and losses as deductions, in the case of single firms and of firms within groups. The latter case is considerably more complex, even with just two firms within a group, and in some cases involves the use of a numerical search procedure. However, this extra complexity is worthwhile, compared with a more mechanical approach, as it is likely to approximate much more closely a net profit minimising, and thus tax minimising, strategy.

Part IV

Corporate Tax Simulations

Chapter 7

Revenue Elasticity Simulations

This chapter presents some results from applying the simulation model CorpSim, described in Part III above. Emphasis is placed on the elasticity of aggregate corporation tax revenue with respect to changes in aggregate gross profits. This is the main summary statistic used to examine fiscal drag. There are many alternative scenarios which could be simulated, including different patterns of profit growth (for example different trend and cycle combinations), different degrees of randomness in the profit growth process and different assumptions regarding correlations both over time and across profit sources. In addition, the proportion of firms in groups could be changed, and the implications of alternative tax rates and thresholds could be investigated.

After briefly describing the simulation procedure in Section 7.1, Section 7.2 considers a benchmark case. Section 7.3 then compares outcomes for alternative values of the key parameters, considering revenue elasticities resulting from larger economic cycles, and the implications of introducing relative movements in profits between firms. Long-run elasticities are examined in Section 7.4. The effects of using an alternative approach to deductions claiming are discussed in Section 7.5.

7.1 The Simulation Procedure

After generating the initial profit distribution, the model is then simulated for 20 periods from $t = 1$, which covers two complete cycles.[1] When examining the single firm case, 20k single firms are drawn from the initial gross A and B profit distributions. It then generates their gross profits for each of the 20 periods and applies eligible deductions to calculate their total taxable or net profits, and hence their corporation tax payments, by applying the appropriate corporation tax rate. Summing across all 20k firms in each period yields the value of total corporation tax payments which, together with the total profits from all firms, allows the revenue elasticity to be calculated using the year-to-year changes.

For the group case, a similar procedure is followed except that 10,000 firms are randomly drawn from each of two separate pairs of profit distributions (for A and B). Selected firms from the first set of draws are then randomly paired with those from the second set. It would be possible to use a non-random pairing procedure but in the absence of clear guidance from theory, or suitable data on the determinants of group membership, the random case provides a useful benchmark. This process essentially determines whether and when groups in the simulation are composed of two profit-makers, two loss-makers, and so on, and the extent of their joint profits or losses.

---

[1]In fact, an initial 10 year period is simulated to allow capital allowances to reach a steady state as discussed below. All results reported below, and referred to as years 1–20, follow that initial 10 year period.

Firms' initial capital allowances are determined by their current investment and their capital allowance pools. Investment is determined from firms' profits using equation (6.2) in Chapter 6. However, with no prior investment, this requires initial capital allowance pools to be specified. This is achieved by setting the ratio of the each firm's initial capital allowance pool to its total gross profit, $CP_{i,1}^A/(P_{i,1}^A + P_{i,1}^B)$, equal to β in (6.2). This has the effect of ensuring that the ratio of the pool of capital allowances to profits available at $t = 1$ is close to the ratio of capital allowances from new investment to profits. Without this assumption, there could be long transition periods until capital allowance pools reached a steady state.

7.2 A Benchmark Case

The following examples begin by considering a benchmark case and then examining variations around that case. Figure 7.1 shows the systematic pattern of the growth rate of average total profit, the sum $P^A + P^B$, both for a relatively low cycle amplitude of 0.005 and for a medium amplitude cycle of 0.01.

The Figure shows 10-year cycles where the low amplitude generates a range of profit growth rates between +3.2 per cent and +0.8 per cent, around a trend of 2 per cent. The medium cycle generates higher growth at the top of the cycle (+4.3 per cent) and growth at the bottom of the cycle that is slightly negative. Both these cycles are examined in section 7.3 which also examines a high cycle amplitude of 0.015, which generates profit growth rates in the range +5.5 per cent to −1.4 per cent. In fact, profit growth rates in practice can fluctuate over a much larger range than even the high-cycle case. The profit growth rates in

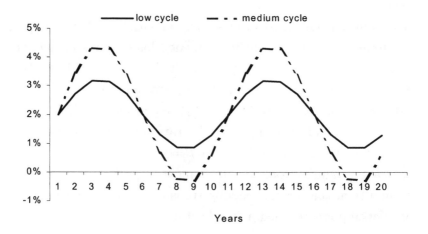

Figure 7.1: Simulated Profit Cycles

Figure 7.1 arise from the combined effect of the assumed trend and cycle in profits, and the trend and cycle in the maximum loss. Profit growth rates of individual firms differ from those average rates to the extent that stochastic processes apply. In the absence of stochastics, all firms have the same growth rates and there are no relative changes in firms' profits.

Benchmark simulations use the low-cycle profit growth shown in Figure 7.1, and abstract from stochastic effects, so that $u_{it}^A = u_{it}^A = 0$. The profit parameters are given in the previous chapter. Benchmark simulations assume a correlation between A and B profits of 0.05. Analysis of around 160,000 firms in the HMRC CT600 database for 2001–02 to 2003–04 produced correlation coefficients in the region of 0.3 to 0.4. Simulations examined include: $\rho = -0.05, 0.0, 0.05$ and 0.40.

Benchmark values for the other parameters in the investment equation, (6.2), are set as follows: $\alpha = 0$; $\beta = 0.15$ (that is, investment is proportional to total current-plus-lagged profits); $\theta = 0.5$ (that is, past and current profits affect investment equally); and $\phi = 0.8$ (that is, B profits take a weight 80 per cent of that for A profits). These weights are not critical for the subsequent results reported, but can readily be altered.

Figure 7.2 shows profit growth and the revenue elasticity for the benchmark case of a low profit cycle (0.8 per cent to 3.2 per cent) and no stochastics, so that all firms move together over the economic cycle. It can be seen that the elasticity fluctuates in what appears to be a counter-cyclical manner, from a minimum of around 1 at high profit growth rates to a maximum of around 1.3 at the lowest point in the cycle. That is, tax growth is up to 30 per cent faster than profit growth at the bottom of the cycle and approximately equal to profit growth at the top of the cycle.

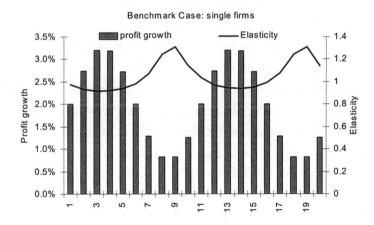

Figure 7.2: Benchmark Case: Single Firms

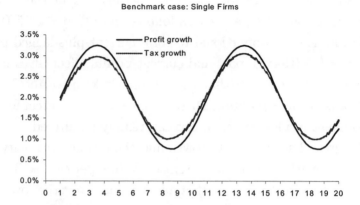

Figure 7.3: Benchmark: Tax and Profit Growth

This result arises because when profit growth falls modestly below trend, the tendency for profits to fall relative to deductions serves to increase the elasticity; that is, tax growth falls proportionately less than profit growth. In this case the cycle is so weak (that is, it has a low amplitude) that the mild downturn causes few firms to move out of taxpaying status.

Figure 7.3 shows the tax and profit growth rates associated with the elasticities in Figure 7.2. This shows that the tax growth profile is a smoothed version of the profit growth profile. Thus tax growth is higher than profit growth at the bottom of the cycle. In understanding this result it is important to remember that total profits here are defined to include negative values (losses), consistent with National Accounting definitions, but unlike the usual HMRC definition of taxable profits. However, tax growth is driven by the growth of positive profit values, which tends to be somewhat more smooth.

Figure 7.4 compares the benchmark elasticity profile for the case where all firms are single with the case where all firms are in groups of two. The group case involves a smoother elasticity profile; in particular, the increase in the elasticity during downturns is less marked. This reflects the fact that, by using group losses contemporaneously to relieve group profits, groups' tax liabilities in aggregate move more in line with their profits (including losses) in aggregate than is possible for single firms.

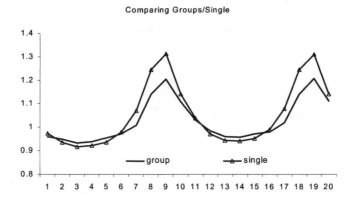

Figure 7.4: Elasticities for Groups and Single Firms: Benchmark case

7.3 Variations from the Benchmark Case

7.3.1 Elasticities with Larger Cycles

The results in Figure 7.4 suggest relatively small elasticities. These are much smaller than the values observed for tax buoyancy, which result in part from the wide fluctuations in profit growth, ranging from almost 20 per cent to -3 per cent per annum. As Figure 7.5 shows, simulating a medium cycle generates quite different elasticity profiles. The medium cycle (with a profit growth range of 4.3 per cent to −0.2 per cent around a 2 per cent trend) produces elasticity profiles that are dramatically different from the benchmark case (requiring a different scale for the vertical axis in Figure 7.5). Most noticeably, the tendency for the elasticity to rise during downturns is essentially reversed in Figure 7.5 with the elasticity dropping close to, or below, zero at the bottom of the recession, but with higher values going into and coming out of the recession.

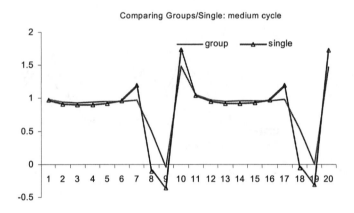

Figure 7.5: Elasticities for Groups and Single Firms with a Medium Cycle

This phenomenon is even more pronounced when a high cycle, with a range of 5.5 per cent to −1.4 per cent combined with a 2 per cent trend, is simulated. This produces elasticities as low as −4 at the bottom of the recession. This reflects the fact that more severe recessions produce many more firms and groups going into loss and hence becoming non-taxpayers, with zero revenue elasticities. Hence tax revenues can fall suddenly even if profit growth remains positive. Equally negative elasticities can arise when recessions generate negative profit growth but tax growth remains positive. This is the case for single firms in Figure 7.5 where the negative profit growth of -0.2 per cent in years 8 and 9 is insufficient to turn tax growth negative, with resulting negative elasticities. Small positive profit growth in year 10 (coming out of the recession) then yields a large positive elasticity. Figure 7.5 also suggests that, apart from during recessionary periods, the elasticity profile is relatively flat around a value of 1.

These results suggest that a regular cyclical process, even without any stochastic effects, can nevertheless produce quite volatile revenue elasticities, moving quickly between positive and negative values in a similar manner to that observed for UK corporate tax buoyancy.

7.3.2 Introducing Relative Profit Changes

In practice there are relative movements of firms within the profit distribution. Many firms can behave differently from the average, either because they make endogenous firm-specific changes with beneficial or adverse consequences for their profit levels, or because they experience unusual exogenous changes which affect their profits. The simulation model captures this by allowing for both random firm-specific profit shocks and the possibility of serial correlation in profits. In the latter case, a higher change in profits in one period may increase, or reduce, the probability of higher changes in profits in subsequent periods; this captures the phenomenon where 'success breeds success'.

To allow the extent to which random effects impact on firms' profits to vary, simulations were carried out using two alternative values for the variance terms, $\sigma_{u_A}^2$, $\sigma_{u_B}^2$. Setting $\sigma_{u_A}^2 = \sigma_{u_B}^2 =$ 0.001 is a relatively high variance, implying a standard deviation of around 3 per cent such that profit growth for about 50 per cent of firms lie outside ± 3 per cent of the mean profit growth rate. That is, at the mid-point of a cycle with trend growth of 2 per cent, around half of all firms experience profit growth outside the -1 per cent to $+5$ per cent range. A lower variance of 0.0002 implies a ± 1.4 per cent band around the mean, so half of all firms profit growth rates lie outside the range from $+0.6$ per cent to $+3.4$ per cent. Clearly, this still represents a fairly high degree of profit variability across firms.

To identify serial correlation within the two income sources of trading and loan-relationship profits, the HMRC CT600 data for 2001-02 to 2003-04 were analysed. This yielded serial correlation values around -0.25 for A profits and -0.2 for B profits. These values are obtained by assuming a first order auto-regressive process for the random component of x_{it}^A and x_{it}^B. Simulations use values of $+0.2$, 0.0 and -0.2 for the serial correlation coefficient.

Figure 7.6 shows the impact on the revenue elasticity of allowing for the high and low variance cases above, with zero serial correlation. These are obtained for the group case with a medium cycle as shown in Figure 7.5. The zero variance case in Figure 7.6 is equivalent to the group case in Figure 7.5; all simulations set serial correlation to zero. It can be seen from Figure 7.6 that allowing for stochastic effects further increases the volatility of the revenue elasticity especially, but not exclusively, during recessions (for example years 8–10). Finally allowing for positive or negative serial correlation (-0.2, $+0.2$) in the random component of profit growth has little effect on the

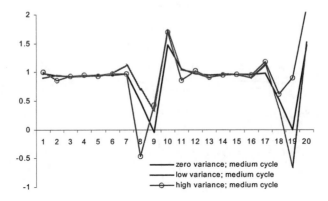

Figure 7.6: Elasticities: Introducing Stochastics

revenue elasticities. In both cases elasticity profiles look similar to those shown in Figure 7.6.

7.3.3 Decomposing the Impact of Deductions

It was shown above that the pro-cyclical nature of capital allowances (because investment is positively correlated with profits) and the counter-cyclical nature of firms' losses implies that these two deductions are expected simultaneously to have differing impacts on the aggregate corporation tax revenue elasticity. It is therefore useful to examine revenue elasticities obtained by setting each of these deductions, in turn, to zero. This effectively decomposes the elasticity into effects due to loss use and group relief growth, and effects due to capital allowance growth. Gross profit growth – the denominator of the elasticity – is the same in each case.

Figure 7.7 repeats the elasticity profile for medium-cycle parameter values, and also shows two decompositions: these are

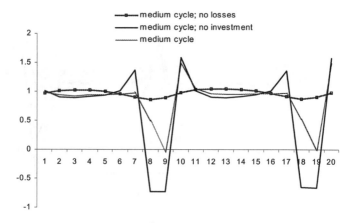

Figure 7.7: Elasticities: Decomposing Deductions

where there is no investment ($\alpha = \beta = 0$ in the investment equation (6.2)) and where there are no losses ($d^A = d^B = 0$). This confirms the expectation that, in the absence of any losses, the pro-cyclical assumption for capital allowances yields a smooth pro-cyclical elasticity profile. On the other hand, if only losses are used as deductions, the elasticity profile closely resembles the overall medium-cycle case. That is, the overall profile is most strongly driven by loss deductions rather than capital allowances. Clearly then, the relative importance of capital allowances and losses used within total deductions has a strong bearing on the cyclical nature of the revenue elasticity. Of course, in practice, investment is not linked to profits in the simple manner depicted here, with profit expectations, interest rates, lags and so on, likely to play a role.

7.3.4 Eliminating the Small Company Rate

This subsection examines the revenue consequences of a change in the tax schedule. However, the outcomes from such exercises should be treated as benchmark simulations of 'impact effects' since behavioural responses to tax changes are excluded. For example, simulating an increase in the main rate would identify the direct revenue effects of the increased tax rate. But it would not take into account potentially important reactions such as changes in reported gross profits in the UK, or firms' responses in the form of additional avoidance schemes to reduce tax liability for a given value of declared profits.

It was suggested above that large firms, paying the 30 per cent rate, account for the major share of receipts, and hence movements across the tax threshold from 19 per cent to 30 per cent would be unlikely to be important for revenue elasticity estimates. This can be tested by setting the tax rate in CorpSim to 30 per cent for all firms above the £10k threshold. Results from this simulation confirm that the elasticity profile is little affected. For example, comparing results with the benchmark case, elasticities at the top of the cycle, where profit growth is 3.2 per cent, for the alternative tax rate scenarios are almost identical at 0.94 and 0.95. Differences are maximised at the bottom of the cycle where profit growth is 0.8 per cent. The benchmark elasticity is 1.20 whilst a value of 1.14 is obtained using a single 30 per cent tax rate for all firms. These differences in the revenue elasticity in the two scenarios arise from the increased revenues predicted when a single 30 per cent tax rate is adopted. Since any behavioural responses would be expected to reduce revenues below this impact effect, the limited responses to the tax change reported here can be regarded as maximum values.

7.4   Revenue Elasticities over the Long Run

The previous section demonstrated the volatility of the corporation tax revenue elasticity over the economic cycle, demonstrating that it can move substantially from year to year in response to changes in profit growth rates. This raises the question of whether, in a world of steady growth, an elasticity value of 1 can be presumed. That is, given the UK corporation tax system, can taxes and profits be expected to grow at the same rate in a steady state? Alternatively, given the existence of economic cycles, and therefore volatile annual revenue elasticities, can the revenue elasticity be expected to average 1 over a complete cycle?

Table 7.1: Elasticities over the Long Run

Simulation		Long-run elasticity	Average elasticity
Benchmark		0.99	1.02
Medium cycle		0.98	0.86
High cycle		0.98	0.15
Low variance	(Low cycle)	0.97	1.02
High variance	(Low cycle)	1.00	1.03
Low variance	(Medium cycle)	0.99	0.95
High variance	(Medium cycle)	1.00	0.83

Table 7.1 shows values for the long-run revenue elasticity, estimated from revenue and gross profit growth over 10 periods (t_1 to t_{10}) – a complete cycle in the model. It also shows an average revenue elasticity: this is the arithmetic average of the 10 annual values of the elasticity, over the same period. The benchmark

case shows that, with low volatility in growth rates (both profits and tax), but no stochastic behaviour, both the elasticity measures approximate 1 (they are 0.99 and 1.02). More volatile behaviour, whether due to greater cyclical effects or stochastic effects, continues to be associated with a long-run elasticity close to 1 but the additional volatility renders the average elasticity value a very poor proxy for the long-run value. Especially with a high cycle, the single large negative annual value, at the bottom of the cycle, dominates the 10-year average.

These results suggest that, despite variability across firms in their profit growth being the norm in practice, over a complete cycle, profit and tax growth are approximately equal. However, given the observed volatility in profit growth rates over time, using averages of annual elasticity values is likely to be misleading.

The simulation model incorporates thousands of firms, each with potentially very different gross profit growth rates such that some firms have zero tax revenue elasticities (non-taxpayers) while others can take a range of positive values greater than 1. Given this, it may seem surprising that the model robustly predicts a long-run revenue elasticity, averaged across all firms, that is so close to 1. However, this result can be explained by recalling that, for unchanged tax rates, tax revenue growth is equal to the growth of net profits (that is, net of all deductions). An elasticity of 1 implies that gross and net profits must be growing at the same rate over the long-run. A sufficient condition for this to occur is that deductions and gross profits grow at the same rate, over the long-run. Since net profit, $P^T = P - D$, then, using a 'dot' over a variable to represent its rate of growth, $\dot{P}^T = \alpha \dot{P} - (1 - \alpha)\dot{D}$, where $\alpha = P/P^T > 1$. If $\dot{P}$ and $\dot{D}$ are equal, they both equal $\dot{P}^T$ independently of the value of α.

This last condition is what might be expected over a complete cycle, and is implicit in the simulation model's assumptions. Over a complete cycle (and especially over several cycles) it would be surprising if investment, and hence capital allowances, were persistently increasing or decreasing relative to profits, though such a pattern might extend for some time. For losses, the other major contributor to deductions, there is no reason to expect those to increase or decrease relative to positive profits over the long run. For example, though losses are expected to worsen relative to profits during a temporary downturn, if they became larger in successive cyclical downturns, it would imply a long-run worsening of profitability in the economy. Such a phenomenon is not typically observed over several cycles.

7.5   Alternative Group Deductions Claiming

This section compares results using the tax minimising assumption with an alternative assumption that groups adopt a fixed order in which available deductions are claimed. In particular, deductions are subtracted in the following order: (i) capital allowances; (ii) current losses are deducted within firms; (iii) excess capital allowances are deducted within firms; (iv) losses are group relieved; (v) losses are brought forward from previous periods and claimed within firms. This order essentially reflects a rule of thumb that current deductions are used within a firm first and are made available to group members only if they cannot be fully used. As with other simulations, past losses are treated as the final deduction to be used because, unlike other deductions, their use is already constrained to be within firms and within schedule.

Figure 7.8 shows the revenue elasticity schedules using the medium cycle and low variance of the random growth component, for both the tax minimising and fixed order cases. It is clear that the method adopted can be important for the measured size of the elasticity. It is more volatile in the fixed order case, especially during recessions, when the fixed order case can reach values of -10.

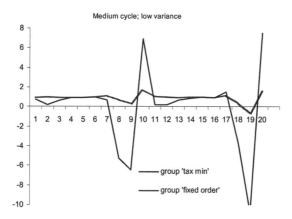

Figure 7.8: Elasticities with Alternative Deduction Methods: Medium Cycle with Low Variance

It is easier to assess what lies behind this result by considering Figure 7.9, which shows profiles for aggregate tax revenues over the 20-year simulation, for the two cases. This indicates, as expected, that the tax minimising profile always lies below the alternative (non-minimising) case. However, it is especially during recessions that tax minimisation makes a strong contribution by allocating losses most efficiently for the group. As

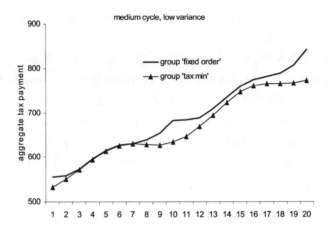

Figure 7.9: Tax Revenue Profiles with Alternative Deduction Methods: Medium Cycle with Low Variance

Figures 7.8 and 7.9 show, failing to do this makes a substantial difference to the levels of tax liability and the elasticity estimates in periods of large losses.

7.6   Conclusions

This chapter has addressed the question of how corporation tax receipts are expected to grow over time, given an unchanged corporation tax regime and compliance effort. Despite the existence of a number of forecasting methods to predict corporation tax revenues (receipts or accruals) this question has previously received surprisingly little attention. This is important for two reasons. First, with growing public expenditure demands, it is necessary for tax authorities to know whether, in the absence of budgetary changes, they can expect improving or worsening revenues from corporation tax both over the longer term and within an economic cycle. Second, if corporation tax revenues can rise or fall without any changes in compliance, but revenue targets are used to assess compliance effort, the ability to meet these will be influenced by factors inherent to the corporation tax system but outside the control of compliance units.

Simulation results suggest a number of conclusions. The growth of aggregate corporation tax revenue appears to be highly volatile in relation to the growth of profits. Volatility in revenue elasticities is generally less when groups can share losses compared with an economy composed only of single firms. Relatively high volatility in revenue elasticities is especially associated with economic downturns, otherwise elasticities tend to hover around a value of 1. This volatility occurs even when all firms' profits are assumed to grow at the same rate, but is exacerbated when random factors allow some firms to deviate from this common growth rate. In mild economic downturns, corporation tax revenue elasticities may rise, because tax growth falls less than profit growth, but in more severe downturns, large but temporary decreases in the revenue elasticity, and even negative elasticities, can be expected.

Capital allowances and losses claimed against positive profits have quite different effects on revenue elasticities, if in general capital allowances are positively correlated (and losses negatively correlated) with profits. Over a full economic cycle, the model suggests plausibly that corporation tax revenues and profits tend to grow at the same rate, in the absence of discretionary changes in tax rates, compliance and so on. However, due to the short-run volatility, annual averages of revenue elasticities are a misleading guide to long-run tax growth.

The empirical analysis of Devereux *et al.* (2004) sought to explain why UK corporation tax revenues had, in general, remained high relative to GDP since the mid-1980s, despite falling statutory corporation tax rates. They concluded that the main factor behind this was the expansion in the share of corporate profits in GDP, mainly associated with financial companies. This therefore expanded the tax base, relative to GDP. The simulation model described here has focused on how revenues change relative to the tax base, suggesting that these are expected to be stable over the long run, but quite unstable in the short run. How the tax base, profits, might change over time requires a separate analysis recognising behavioural factors, including the potential for the tax regime itself to influence firms' profitability and how and where their profits are declared for tax purposes.

Although many simplifications were required in constructing and calibrating the microsimulation model CorpSim, it is able to capture many of the crucial features of the distribution of profits in the UK and their relative movements. The simulation results have demonstrated the value of producing a model of this kind, in view of its ability to generate valuable insights into the behaviour of corporation tax revenue elasticities.

Chapter 8

Tax Response Simulations

This chapter examines the impact of profit-offsetting deductions on firms' choices to shift profits or real activity out of their home tax jurisdiction. This is a hitherto neglected aspect in the empirical literature on investment relocation and profit shifting by firms when corporate tax rates change. Profit shifting or income shifting refers to the phenomenon whereby the location of economic activity is unchanged but the extent to which any resulting profits or incomes are declared in home or foreign tax jurisdictions changes. In particular, the chapter explores the importance of the endogenous relationship between deductions and profits and the consequences of asymmetries in the tax treatment of profits and losses.

A variety of methods and datasets have produced quite a wide range of estimates of international profit shifting or real investment responses; see, for example, Grubert and Mutti (1991), Hines and Rice (1994), Grubert and Slemrod (1998), Demirgüç-Kunt and Huizinga (2001), Markusen (2002), Devereux and Hubbard (2003), Bartelsman and Beetsma (2003) and Huizinga and Laeven (2007). Of course, profit responses to corporate tax changes are not confined to multinational firms. They can also be expected for purely domestic firms when increases in tax rates reduce net-of-tax profits at the margin and so render some previously profitable production unprofitable. In some cases firms may change to non-corporate status in response to differences in personal and corporate income tax regimes.

All firms' corporation tax liabilites are affected by deductions to some degree, of which past losses and investment allowances are typically the most prominent. In the UK, for example, on average corporate taxable profits after deductions are approximately half of gross (before deductions) profits. Those deductions that are loss-related often display a strong cyclical component. This reflects, in part, their asymmetric treatment under the tax code: losses typically do not attract an immediate tax rebate equivalent to the tax rate on positive profits. For the US, Auerbach (2007) shows that differences between observed (implicit) average and statutory rates of corporate income tax are substantively due to the asymmetric treatment of losses for tax purposes. This appears to account for a large fraction of cyclical changes in implicit average tax rates and the observed trend towards higher implicit average rates (despite a declining statutory rate) in the US since the early 1980s. This leads Auerbach to query whether tax-sheltering of profits is as important as suggested in much of the empirical literature. Auerbach's analysis uses an extended version of the Auerbach and Poterba (1987) methodology that decomposes differences in statutory and observed average tax rates into the effects associated with capital depreciation, inflationary effects, tax losses, and foreign income sources.

That empirical literature has largely relied on profit data from commercial or National Account sources, which inevitably restricts the extent to which the impact of 'deductions shifting', or the constraints that deductions eligibility places on profit shifting, can be explored. Auerbach's (2007) analysis, on the other hand, is possible because of the availability of taxpayer gross profit and deductions data. To explore the role of deductions in profit-shifting estimates, this chapter uses the CorpSim microsimulation model of the UK corporate tax system described in Part III of this book. This model was designed to explore the impact of tax losses and capital allowances on companies' profits net of deductions. Here it is used, in conjunction with a decomposition of a standard profit responsiveness elasticity, described below, to identify the likely impact on that elasticity of allowing for endogenous deductions and tax loss asymmetries.

Section 8.1 begins with a simple model of a corporate tax system applied at the firm level, examining how profits and deductions can be expected to vary over the business cycle. Section 8.2 defines firms' behavioural responses and shows how they can be decomposed into real, profit-shifting and deductions-shifting components. Section 8.3 discusses the basic assumptions used in the simulations. Section 8.4 reports resulting numerical values for aggregate elasticities based on simulating a profit cycle around a trend. Section 8.5 reports several sensitivity analyses.

8.1   A Simple Corporate Tax Model

This section provides a simplified model of a single corporation (referred to hereafter as a 'firm') which is located in a given tax jurisdiction. The firm may, at some cost, change its declared profits in that jurisdiction in response to a change in the jurisdiction's tax rate. For comparative static purposes, tax rates in

other jurisdictions are assumed throughout to be independent
of the tax rate in the host country; hence responses to a change
in this jurisdiction's tax rate can be interpreted as responses to
a change in the tax differential. The aim is to obtain an initial indication of the effect on the firm's behaviour of variations
in profits over the economic cycle. Subsection 8.1.1 specifies the
composition of a firm's net taxable profits. Subsection 8.1.2 then
considers the factors likely to impact on the cyclical pattern of
deductions claiming.

8.1.1   Taxable Profits and Deductions

Define P_j and D_j respectively as the firm's gross profits and
deductions available to offset gross profits in year j.[1] In the
UK, the main expenditures which qualify as deductions are investment expenditures subject to fiscal depreciation rules and
accumulated losses. The deductions value of each of these depends on certain qualifying conditions which limit or extend the
generosity of their fiscal value. Gross profits declared for tax
in year j can be similarly defined as P_j^*, and total deductions
claimed against those declared profits are D_j^*, so that net taxable
profits in j, P_j^T, are:

$$P_j^T = P_j^* - D_j^* \tag{8.1}$$

Equation (8.1) applies to a single year, though the deductions
can include unused eligible expenditures and losses carried forward from previous periods. As discussed in further detail be-

---

[1]Gross profits in this context are those defined by the tax authorities as liable to tax,
before any deductions. It includes profits from all types of taxable income such as trading
profits and investment profits. This typically differs from standard accounting definitions,
such as EBITDA (earnings before interest, taxes, depreciation and amortisation), for example in its treatment of interest payments.

low, some deductions are related to profits, hence $D_j^* = D_j(P_j^*)$, but the short form is used here. Considering, for simplicity, a single corporate tax rate of t, tax liability, $T_j\left(P_j^*\right)$, is given by:

$$
\begin{aligned}
T_j\left(P_j^*\right) &= 0 & \text{if } P_j^T \leq 0 \\
&= tP_j^T = t\left(P_j^* - D_j^*\right) & \text{if } P_j^T > 0 \quad (8.2)
\end{aligned}
$$

where $0 \leq D_j^* \leq P_j^*$; that is, only an amount of currently available deductions up to the value of current declared profit can be claimed against those profits.

It is this asymmetric feature of the UK and many other countries' corporate tax systems, whereby available deductions do not give rise to a direct tax rebate when they exceed current declared profits, that contributes to an endogenous response of deductions to profits. Instead losses are typically deductible, subject to various restrictions, against past, current or future positive profits within the firm, or groups of associated firms.

In the UK system, for example, a current loss under one profit schedule or source may be offset against a current profit under some, but not all, other schedules. Losses can generally be carried forward within schedule indefinitely but carried back only one year. Firms which form part of a group may alternatively transfer losses within the group but only concurrently. Thus a firm's ability to utilise its losses immediately can depend on the schedular characteristics of its profits and losses. Simulating the dynamic pattern of deductions in section 8.4 shows that this asymmetry plays an important role in affecting the behaviour of revenue elasticities over the business cycle. First, the following subsection uses a simple conceptual approach to assess the cyclical properties of capital allowance and loss deductions, in the absence of any tax rate changes.

8.1.2   Deductions over the Cycle

Capital allowances available to be claimed in year j are denoted by A_j. To simplify the exposition, assume straightline depreciation at a rate of δ per year over $i = 0, ..., n$ years, where n is the terminal year. Thus, if I_{j-i} is qualifying investment undertaken in year $j - i$:

$$A_j = \delta \left[I_j + I_{j-1} + I_{j-2}...I_{j-n} \right] = \delta \sum_{i=0}^{n} I_{j-i} \qquad (8.3)$$

Assuming that investment in a given year is a simple positive function of declared gross profit in that year,[2] such that $I_{j-i} = \pi_{j-i} P_{j-i}^*$, (8.3) can be rewritten as:

$$A_j = \delta \sum_{i=0}^{n} \pi_{j-i} P_{j-i}^* \qquad (8.4)$$

Capital allowances claimed in a given year, A_j^*, are determined by the availability of both declared gross profits in that year and the accumulated pool of capital allowances (unclaimed from previous years), such that:

$$\begin{aligned} A_j^* &= 0 & \text{if } P_j^* \leq 0 \\ &= \min\left(A_j, P_j^*\right) & \text{if } P_j^* > 0 \qquad (8.5) \end{aligned}$$

where A_j is given by (8.4). That is, provided there are positive declared gross profits in j, capital allowances may be claimed up to the value of those allowances or declared gross profits, whichever is the smaller.

---

[2]This relationship reflects the observation that investment tends to be higher when company profits are higher. A structure of lagged πs can be added here but would complicate the exposition without adding additional insight.

A similar situation exists for deductions associated with past losses. Define the pool of accumulated, unclaimed past losses available to be used as deductions in j as L_j, and losses claimed in year j are L_j^*. As in the UK system it is also assumed that capital allowances are claimed first against gross profits, with loss pools claimed against any remaining (positive) profits net of capital allowances. Thus loss deductions claimed are simply:

$$L_j^* = 0 \qquad\qquad\qquad\qquad \text{if } P_j^* - A_j^* \leq 0$$
$$= \min\left(L_j, P_j^* - A_j^*\right) \qquad \text{if } P_j^* - A_j^* > 0 \quad (8.6)$$

Hence total deductions available in year j are given by $D_j = A_j + L_j$, while deductions actually claimed against gross profits are $D_j^* = A_j^* + L_j^*$. To assess cyclical properties of these claimed deductions, A_j^* and L_j^*, in response to changes in declared gross profits, it is helpful to consider the partial derivatives, dA_j^*/dP_j^*, and dA_j^*/dP_{j-i}^* $(i > 0)$, and equivalent derivatives for losses. These respectively capture the current and lagged responses of the two deductions to changes in declared gross profits.

Table 8.1 below shows three phases associated with capital allowance claiming: a 'recession' phase, when $P_j^* < 0$; a 'recovery' phase, when gross profits are positive but less than available deductions, $0 < P_j^* < D_j$; and a 'boom' phase when $P_j^* > D_j$, such that positive net taxable profits are earned. There are equivalent phases for loss claims except that for this case $P_j^* A_j$ is required rather than $P_j^* 0$. That is, to the extent that firms have capital allowances, movement into recovery or boom phases for loss deductions would be delayed relative to capital allowance claims.

Even for capital allowance deductions, these phases do not necessarily correspond with troughs and peaks in profit levels since positive net taxable profits $(P_j^* > D_j)$ may arise, following a period of losses, before or after a gross profit peak is reached or may indeed persist throughout a trough in gross profit levels. Similarly, during downswings towards a recession phase, net taxable profits may remain positive $(P_j^* > D_j)$. However, the three phases correspond to different qualifying conditions affecting a company's tax liability, with either gross or net profits increasing from recession, through recovery, to boom phases.

Table 8.1: Cyclical Responses of Deductions

Capital allowances:	Recession $(P_j^* < 0)$	Recovery $(0 < P_j^* < D_j)$	Boom $(P_j^* > D_j)$
1. dA_j^*/dP_j^*	0	1	$\delta\pi_j$
2. dA_j^*/dP_{j-1}^*	0	[positive]	[positive]
Losses:	$(P_j^* < A_j)$	$(A_j < P_j^* < D_j)$	$(P_j^* > D_j)$
3. dL_j^*/dP_j^*	0	1	0
4. dL_j^*/dP_{j-1}^*	0	$[+ve$ or $-ve]$	[negative]

Table 8.1 shows derivatives for the current period, j, and the previous period, $j - 1$: as explained below, these illustrate the assumption of positive first-order serial correlation in successive profit changes, such that $dP_j^*/dP_{j-1}^* > 0$.[3] First, in the recession phase – when gross profits are negative – there can be no changes to claimed deductions. Second, in a recovery phase, a unit increase in current declared gross profits $(dP_j^* > 0$; see lines 1 and 3) generates a unit increase in either loss or capital allowance deductions claimed, since in such phases, these are constrained by current declared gross profits rather than the de-

---

[3]Results for the derivatives in Table 8.1 assume that the modelled increase in gross profits does not push the firm into a different phase.

ductions available. Third, in a boom phase a unit increase in P_j^* gives rise to a direct increase in capital allowance deductions equal to $\delta\pi_j > 0$, reflecting the deductions value in year j of the additional investment, I_j, generated by the additional unit of current declared gross profit, P_j^*. The contemporaneous effects on capital allowances of higher gross profits are therefore all zero or positive, confirming generally positive co-movement with gross profits, though these could be higher in recovery than boom phases, due to large pools of unused allowances available in the former.

For the lagged responses, line 2 shows that the response of capital allowance deductions claimed to changes in lagged declared gross profit is positive in both recovery and boom phases. This can be seen by noting that the overall response reflects both a direct and an indirect response. Thus dA_j^*/dP_{j-1}^* can be decomposed as follows:

$$\frac{dA_j^*}{dP_{j-1}^*} = \left.\frac{\partial A_j^*}{\partial P_{j-1}^*}\right|_{dP_j^*=0} + \left[\frac{\partial A_j^*}{\partial P_j^*}\right]\left[\frac{dP_j^*}{dP_{j-1}^*}\right] \qquad (8.7)$$

$$= \quad \text{positive} \quad + \quad [1 \text{ or } \delta\pi_j] \,[\text{positive}]$$

This expression captures the positive direct effect on current capital allowance deductions of lagged profit changes (via the higher persisting fiscal depreciation arising from higher lagged investment) plus an indirect effect to the extent that current and lagged values of gross profits are correlated (that is, $dP_j^*/dP_{j-1}^* \neq 0$). For the case of positive first-order serial correlation – perhaps the most plausible assumption regarding observed cyclical behaviour – equation (8.7) confirms a positive relationship in both recovery and boom phases; that is, $\delta\pi_j > 0$.

Hence capital allowance deductions might be expected to

display broadly pro-cyclical behaviour in the absence of tax rate changes and any associated behavioural responses to these. However, as stressed above, this pro-cyclical pattern in terms of broad phases of gross profit levels need not coincide with peaks and troughs in the cycle. For example, a severe recession with several years of negative declared gross profits could give rise to a prolonged subsequent recovery phase when $0 < P_j^* < D_j$, beyond a subsequent peak in declared gross profit levels, P_j^*. In addition, as line 2 of Table 8.1 shows, the increase in capital allowance deductions when gross profits rise in the recovery period could be greater than in a boom if $\delta\pi_j < 1$. In practice, pro-cyclicality in capital allowance deductions might be expected to be further reduced by the long fiscal depreciation regime for some capital items such as structures and buildings, which are typically depreciated over 25 years or more. This tends to dampen annual fluctuation in the stock of depreciation allowances.

The responses of loss deductions to an increase in lagged declared gross profits shown in line 4 of Table 8.1 are obtained from considering the sign of the derivative in the following expression:

$$\frac{dL_j^*}{dP_{j-1}^*} = \left.\frac{\partial L_j^*}{\partial P_{j-1}^*}\right|_{dP_j^*=0} + \left[\frac{\partial L_j^*}{\partial P_j^*}\right]\left[\frac{dP_j^*}{dP_{j-1}^*}\right] \tag{8.8}$$

$$= \quad \text{negative} \quad + \quad [1 \text{ or } 0]\ [\text{positive}]$$

In this case, unlike capital allowances, the direct effect of higher lagged declared gross profits is lower loss deductions claimed because, *certeris paribus*, more of any pre-existing loss pools have been used in $j-1$. However, the indirect effect is positive or zero, depending on the phase under consideration. In particular, in a recovery, $\partial L_j^*/\partial P_j^* = 1$, and an additional unit of losses from pre-existing loss pools can be claimed for every additional unit of gross profit. In a boom, $\partial L_j^*/\partial P_j^* = 0$ and all loss pools are already fully exhausted. Therefore, the overall lagged response of loss deductions claimed, dL_j^*/dP_{j-1}^*, is ambiguous in recoveries and negative in booms.

These results for losses suggest that, although no loss deductions are claimed in recessions, when there are no declared gross profits to offset, loss deduction claiming might be expected to exhibit a form of delayed counter-cyclical pattern such that they rise in recovery phases but fall in booms. In aggregate, even severe recessions are associated with some firms remaining in profit and hence able to use off-setting deductions.

8.2 Decomposing Behavioural Elasticities

The previous section showed that responses of declared deductions (that is, claimed) to changes in declared profits reflect the endogenous properties of the relationships between gross profits, capital allowances and losses. This section considers the implications of this endogeneity for the size of the elasticity of tax revenue with respect to the tax rate. However, it is first necessary to show that it is sufficient in a proportional tax structure to concentrate attention on the responsiveness of net taxable profits (declared gross profits net of declared deductions) to changes in the corporate tax rate.

For a firm with positive net taxable profits, the change in tax revenue, T, as the tax rate varies is given, from (8.2), by $dT/dt = P^T + t \, dP^T/dt$. Using the form, $\eta_{x,y} = (dx/dy)(y/x)$ to denote the elasticity of x with respect to y, the elasticity of T

with respect to t can be written as:

$$\eta_{T,t} = 1 + \eta_{P^T,t} \tag{8.9}$$

where $\eta_{P^T,t} \leq 0$ is the elasticity of net taxable profit, P^T, with respect to the tax rate. Hence the remainder of this chapter focuses on this 'tax base' elasticity, $\eta_{P^T,t}$. The concept is related to the Feldstein (1995) elasticity of taxable income with respect to the net-of-tax or retention rate, $1 - t$, such that $\eta_{P^T,t} = -\left(\frac{t}{1-t}\right)\eta_{P^T,1-t}$.

8.2.1   A Decomposition

Allowing for behavioural responses requires the extent to which profits and deductions are claimed in a given tax jurisdiction to be specified. Define θ_p as the proportion of gross profits, P, declared in the jurisdiction, so that $P^* = \theta_p P$. Furthermore, let θ_d denote the proportion of available deductions which are declared in the jurisdiction, so that $D^* = \theta_d D$. Hence, net taxable profit in the jurisdiction, P^T, can be rewritten as:

$$P^T = \theta_p P - \theta_d D \tag{8.10}$$

To the extent that a firm's gross profits or deductions change in response to changes in taxes, while keeping constant the proportion declared for tax in the jurisdiction, these are defined here as 'real', and are characterised by $\eta_{P,t} \neq 0$ and $\eta_{D,t} \neq 0$ respectively Alternatively, where total profits or deductions remain unchanged but the proportion declared alters, profit or deductions shifting is considered to have occurred, and $\eta_{\theta_p,t} \neq 0$ and $\eta_{\theta_d,t} \neq 0$.[4]

---

[4]The term 'deductions shifting' here is used to capture the opportunity for available

Differentiating P^T with respect to t, it can be shown after some rearrangement that:

$$\eta_{P^T,t} = \alpha \left\{ \eta_{\theta_p,t} + \eta_{P,t} \right\} + (1-\alpha) \left\{ \eta_{\theta_d,t} + \eta_{D,t} \right\} \qquad (8.11)$$

where $\alpha = \theta_p P/P^T = P^*/P^T$ denotes the ratio of declared gross profits to the tax base. This is strictly greater than 1 as long as there are some declared deductions, which in turn requires the firm to have positive declared gross profits. Hence $\alpha - 1 = \theta_d D/P^T = D^*/P^T$ is the ratio of declared deductions to the tax base.

Equation (8.11) provides the basic decomposition of the elasticity of the tax base, net taxable profit, with respect to the tax rate for a single firm. The term $\eta_{\theta_p,t} + \eta_{P,t}$ measures profit responses (shifting and real respectively) while the second term $\eta_{\theta_d,t} + \eta_{D,t}$ measures deductions responses. Thus the elasticity of net taxable profit with respect to the tax rate, $\eta_{P^T,t}$, is a weighted average of profit and deductions elasticities. Given that the elasticity of *declared* gross profits, $\eta_{P^*,t}$, is equal to $\eta_{\theta_p,t} + \eta_{P,t}$, much of the empirical debate over profit shifting, depending on the precise data used, can be seen as providing measures of $\eta_{P^*,t}$ or the elasticity of the proportion declared, $\eta_{\theta_p,t}$.[5]

In the analysis below it is assumed that $\eta_{\theta_p,t} \leq 0$ and $\eta_{P,t} < 0$, so that substitution effects dominate income effects, which accords with the finding of Gruber and Saez (2002) and others that compensated and uncompensated taxable income elasticities are

---

deductions not declared in the host jurisdiction to be transferred to another jurisdiction. In any given time period, not all such available deductions may actually be shifted abroad; some may remain undeclared (unclaimed) in either jurisdiction. They therefore remain available to be claimed or shifted abroad in a subsequent period.

[5] However, Dwenger and Steiner (2008) provide an estimate for Germany of a taxable profit elasticity which takes account of loss deductions.

similar. Negative $\eta_{P,t}$ could reflect both real resources shifting abroad and reductions in domestic activity due to the lower post-tax rates of return, relative to current levels abroad and previous domestic levels respectively. Similarly for $\eta_{\theta_p,t}$, whereby profit shifting may include domestic firms shifting profits out of the corporate tax regime and into alternative taxes (or no tax, via evasion).

A higher proportion of deductions claimed in the jurisdiction might be expected to arise from increased tax rates; hence $\eta_{\theta_d,t} > 0$. Therefore the two profit responses, $\eta_{\theta_p,t}$ and $\eta_{P,t}$, appear to encourage a negative value of $\eta_{PT,t}$ and are compounded by further negative effects on $\eta_{PT,t}$ from the deductions response, $\eta_{\theta_d,t}$.

8.2.2   Endogenous Deduction Responses

Equation (8.11) treats profits and deductions available as profit offsets as independent when, as section 8.1 showed, they may often be expected to be related. Some business expenditures qualifying as deductions, such as capital expenditures, may be correlated with profits while others such as losses are directly profit-related. Hence there may be some endogenous or 'automatic' response of deductions to tax-induced changes in declared gross profits. For example, if a firm transfers production out of a host country in response to a tax change, a gross profit stream that would have been earned and declared in that country is now earned abroad. The associated investment which shifts abroad, previously deductible from host profits, is no longer deductible. Similar arguments apply to losses: the deductions value of past losses depends on current or future profits declared in the same tax jurisdiction, as emphasised in the Auerbach and Poterba (1987) and Auerbach (2007) analyses.

Hence, consider deductions, D, as a function of t and P, and hold other variables such as θ_d and θ_p constant. To simplify the exposition, it is assumed that $\eta_{\theta_p,P} = \eta_{\theta_d,P} = 0$, so that the proportion of gross profits declared for tax purposes is invariant with respect to the level of a firm's profits. This assumption may readily be altered, but at the cost of increasing the number of unobservable parameters for which values must be imposed.

Total differentiation gives $dD = \frac{\partial D}{\partial t}dt + \frac{\partial D}{\partial P}dP$, or in elasticity form:

$$\eta_{D,t} = \eta'_{D,t} + \left(\eta'_{D,P}\right)\left(\eta_{P,t}\right) \qquad (8.12)$$

where a prime is used to indicate a partial elasticity. The right-hand side of (8.12) contains two partial elasticities. The term $\eta'_{D,t} = \frac{t}{D}\frac{\partial D}{\partial t}$ captures the ability of firms to generate deductions that are not related to gross profit levels. These are referred to below as 'autonomous deductions'. Further, $\eta'_{D,P} = \frac{P}{D}\frac{\partial D}{\partial P}$ represents the extent to which deductions change endogenously as profits change, as discussed above. The relative sizes of the components in (8.12) are likely to be affected both by changes in firms' economic circumstances and by tax rules.

In general the sign of $\eta_{D,t}$ is ambiguous. Consider the first term on the right hand side of (8.12). Companies can be expected to increase autonomous deductions in response to an increase in the tax rate since their fiscal value as profit offsets is increased: thus $\eta'_{D,t} > 0$. As argued above, $\eta_{P,t} < 0$. However, the size and sign of the endogenous response component, $\eta'_{D,P}$, depends on a number of factors.

First, the type of deductions-qualifying expenditure is likely to be important. Higher investment may give rise to both higher profits and deductions (capital allowances). But higher loss-related deductions are likely to be associated with generally lower profits in previous and/or current periods. Second, whether changes in P^* arise from changes in total profits, P, or changes in profit shifting, θ_p, may be relevant. Changes in real profit-generating activities might be expected to generate associated deductions more easily than when profits are artificially shifted, since the former may be easier to justify as genuinely deductible. In addition, where the tax code induces a greater endogenous response via $(\eta'_{D,P})(\eta_{P,t})$, firms may compensate with a larger autonomous shifting response, $\eta'_{D,t}$. For example, if a tax rise leads to investment and the associated profits relocating abroad, firms may attempt to compensate for the loss of capital allowances in one jurisdiction by shifting other deductions into that tax jurisdiction; see subsection 8.5.3 for further discussion.

Substituting the expression for $\eta_{D,t}$ in (8.12) into (8.11) gives:

$$\eta_{PT,t} = \alpha \left\{ \eta_{\theta_p,t} + \eta_{P,t} \right\} + (1 - \alpha) \left\{ \eta_{\theta_d,t} + \eta'_{D,t} + \left(\eta'_{D,P} \right) \left(\eta_{P,t} \right) \right\} \tag{8.13}$$

Equation (8.13) could be used to examine the relative importance of endogenous deduction responses, compared with gross profit responses, real and shifting. However, data available for microsimulation relate to declared profits, P^*, rather than P. Thus, it is necessary to express (8.13) in terms of P^*. Using the general properties of elasticities it can be shown that:

$$\eta'_{D,P} = \eta'_{D,P^*} \eta'_{P^*,P} \tag{8.14}$$

and

$$\eta_{P,t} = \frac{\eta_{P^*,t}}{\eta_{P^*,P}} \tag{8.15}$$

Further, from the assumption above that $\eta_{\theta_p,P} = \eta_{\theta_d,P} = 0$, then $\eta_{P*,P} = \eta'_{P*,P} = 1$, and substituting (8.14) and (8.15) into (8.13) yields;

$$\eta_{PT,t} = \alpha \left\{ \eta_{\theta_p,t} + \eta_{P,t} \right\} + (1 - \alpha) \left\{ \eta_{\theta_d,t} + \eta'_{D,t} + \left(\eta'_{D,P*} \right) \left(\eta_{P*,t} \right) \right\}$$
(8.16)

Equation (8.16) is the decomposition used to simulate the behavioural responses of profit and deductions in section 8.4.

Values of $\eta_{PT,t}$ may be expected to differ between, for example, large and small firms, or domestic and multinational firms. However, for tax policy purposes *aggregate* elasticities across all firms are more relevant. To distinguish aggregate from individual firms' elasticities, the notation $\Omega_{x,y}$ is used to denote the aggregate equivalent of $\eta_{x,y}$. It can be shown that $\Omega_{PT,t}$ is a weighted average of the individual values of $\eta_{PT,t}$ with weights given by the taxable profit share of firm i, $\left(P_i^T / \sum_i P_i^T \right)$. The aggregate form of equation (8.16) thus becomes:

$$\Omega_{PT,t} = \alpha \left\{ \Omega_{\theta_p,t} + \Omega_{P,t} \right\} + (1-\alpha) \left\{ \Omega_{\theta_d,t} + \Omega'_{D,t} + \left(\Omega'_{D,P*} \right) \left(\Omega_{P*,t} \right) \right\}$$
(8.17)

where $\Omega_{\theta_p,t} + \Omega_{P,t} = \Omega_{P*,t}$ is the aggregate declared profit response. The following section examines empirical estimates in the profit-shifting literature which appear to capture at least some of the elements of equation (8.17).

8.3   Simulation Model Properties

CorpSim generates simulated initial distributions for each of the two main profit sources – trading profits and interest income – across firms. As explained in Part III of this book, these are fitted to the actual distributions using a mixture of lognormal distributions, suitably adjusted to produce negative profit values. The ability of CorpSim to match the actual Lorenz curves for firms' (positive) profits and losses was demonstrated in Part III.

It is also important that deductions claimed, relative to profits are suitably captured by the simulation model, since this affects the accuracy of simulated values of α. This depends on the size of both losses claimed and capital allowances. The modelling of capital allowances is discussed further below, but as a further check, the simulated values of α, were compared with HMRC equivalents. The observed values for 2003 and 2004 are 2.25 and 2.20 respectively; equivalent values produced by CorpSim are around 2.08. Actual values of this ratio tend to fluctuate depending on the stage of the cycle and sectoral composition. For example, $P^*/P^T = 2.11$ in 2000 for companies in aggregate, but was only 1.93 for financial companies and 2.19 for non-financial companies.

Firms in CorpSim undertake investment which, given fiscal depreciation rules, determines the value of their capital allowances. The model adopts a reduced form investment function in which investment in each period is a positive function of past and current profits (both trading profit and interest income). Though this is clearly not a satisfactory model of the determinants of investment, the key requirement here is that it captures a positive correlation between investment and profits. One rationale for such a correlation is that imperfect capital markets lead firms to prefer internal sources of finance for investment projects. Though the investment function does not include tax parameters directly, to the extent that profits or deductions declared at home are affected by t (and s), investment, and hence capital allowances, are affected.

Finally, the UK tax code allows firms to share some losses concurrently with others in the same corporate group; but these cannot subsequently be carried forward or back. This complicates tax loss asymmetries and is accommodated within the model by allocating firms to groups. CorpSim does not attempt to endogenise group formation. Instead, firms are allocated randomly to groups of two, except for those large profit-making firms generated from an upper tail of a simulated profit distribution, which are matched randomly with firms making large losses. That is, though most firms are grouped randomly so that two profit-making, two loss-making or loss-profit combinations may arise, large profit makers are grouped only with large loss makers. The matching of large profit and loss makers accounts for 12 per cent of the total firm pairs in the sample, and captures the empirical reality that firms with very large losses are almost always observed within groups with large profits elsewhere.

Despite this simplification, with two profit sources and two firms in a group there are ten different resulting profit and loss combinations possible. CorpSim employs a range of algorithms to ensure that, given the configuration of group members' profits and losses, deductions are allocated within the group in a tax-minimising way, subject to tax code restrictions. Allowing for more than two group members would considerably complicate this tax-minimising procedure. The two-firm group structure nevertheless captures the essential characteristic required here that a fraction of a firm's current losses may be used in the year they arise by transferring them to profitable group members.

8.3.1 Behavioural Response Estimates

The decomposition in equation (8.17) requires values for the autonomous profit and deductions responses chosen by firms. The current literature has not explicitly estimated deduction-shifting elasticities but has produced a range of values from which either overall (real plus shifting) or shifting-only profit responses can be derived. In some cases these may implicitly include some deductions shifting. For example, profit-shifting estimates are typically based on commercial data for pre-tax profits. These profit data will normally have been derived after accounting for various expenditures that are deductable for tax purposes as well as some that are not.

Estimates for various profit-shifting responses for samples of multinational corporations have been reported by, for example, Hines and Rice (1994), Grubert and Slemrod (1998), Demirgüç-Kunt and Huizinga (2001), Bartelsman and Beetsma (2003) and Huizinga and Laeven (2007). These typically report 'substantial' profit-shifting responses, measured by changes in either a pre-tax profit measure or tax revenues, in association with tax rate changes. Unfortunately, these can not always readily be compared with elasticities such as the $\Omega_{PT,t}$ used here. However, Bartelsman and Beetsma (2003) report an estimated elasticity of declared tax revenue with respect to the tax rate, for OECD countries, $\Omega_{T,t}$ around 0.35. From (8.9), since $\Omega_{PT,t} = \Omega_{T,t} - 1$, the implied tax base elasticity is -0.65. Bartelsman and Beetsma also obtained UK-specific parameter estimates of similar size. By focusing only on shifting responses they suggest that their estimates could be regarded as lower bounds.

Recent estimates for European multinationals, from Huizinga and Laeven (2007), are somewhat smaller for the UK than those derived from the Bartelsman and Beetsma results. They report a the semi-elasticity of declared pre-tax profits with respect to the top statutory tax rate of around 1.1 for the UK and 1.4 for Europe on average. Taking these as estimates of $d \ln P^T / dt$, and using a 30 per cent corporate tax rate, would suggest elasticities of -0.33 and -0.43 respectively. However, the Huizinga and Laeven semi-elasticities are based on profits data in commercial accounts and are not necessarily equivalent to the elasticity measured here which relates to net taxable profits. Earlier estimates by Demirgüç-Kunt and Huizinga (2001) of profit shifting by multinational banks, essentially found there was no significant change in their domestic tax payments when domestic tax rates increased, implying $\Omega_{T,t} = 0$ or $\Omega_{PT,t} = -1$. Domestic banks revealed a statistically insignificant positive response in their tax liabilities to tax rate changes, but which was statistically larger than the negative (and insignificantly different from zero) response by foreign banks.

These results essentially confirm the evidence of Hines and Rice (1994) who focused on aggregate reported profits of US parents and affiliates with investments in tax havens and other foreign countries. They found that a 1 percentage point higher tax rate reduced reported profits by 3 per cent. Across such a wide-ranging sample of countries, the corporate tax rate is likely to vary, but using an average of around 30 per cent implies a tax base elasticity around -1, while a 15 per cent tax rate implies an elasticity around -0.5. Clausing (2009) reports more wide-ranging results for US multinationals and finds that a 1 percentage point higher corporate tax rate is associated with a profit rate (defined as the ratio of gross profits to sales) lower by 0.5 percentage points.

In summary the existing empirical literature has produced estimates of profit-shifting elasticities or semi-elasticities that might be interpreted as responses of a form of gross or 'net' profit to changes in tax rates, though the profit measures considered generally rely on some form of commercial accounting data for which profit definitions can be quite different from tax accounting equivalents. For example, commercial accounts typically capture only a fraction of the relevant tax deductions in a given year. They may capture fiscal depreciation reasonably well but, importantly, often do not reflect deductions associated with loss carry forwards. As a result, previous profit-shifting estimates may be a better proxy for the autonomous profit-shifting component of the model, $\Omega_{\theta_p,t}$, rather than $\Omega_{P^*,t}$, or $\Omega_{P^T,t}$.

How elasticities might differ between gross profit shifting and deduction shifting is, however, largely unknown. There are also few estimates that formally distinguish real from shifting responses, though several recent studies have stressed that profit-shifting responses may be much larger than real responses.[6] Some real responses may be captured within profit-shifting results. For example Grubert and Slemrod (1998) and Clausing (2009) suggest that profit-shifting and real investment responses are close complements so that both effects may be highly correlated. Clausing (2009) also attempts to separate real from profit-shifting responses by using employment data to proxy the former. She finds a real (employment) response parameter less than a third the size of the overall profit response and concludes

---

[6]See, for example, Harris (1993), Slemrod (1995), Kemsley (1998), Gordon and Slemrod (1998), Gresik (2001), Carroll and Hrung (2005), Clausing (2009).

(2009, p. 717) that revenue effects from shifting profits are 'more than twice as large' as real responses. Further, she argues that this probably represents an upper bound for the relative size of real responses since an unknown fraction of real reactions are driven by profit-shifting motives.

Overall, estimated magnitudes for some form of profit-shifting elasticity in OECD countries appear to be of the order of -0.3 or less, but are generally unlikely to be less than -1. The following subsection discusses a range of parameter values used in simulations that are consistent with $\Omega_{\theta_p,t}$, $\Omega_{P*,t}$, or $\Omega_{PT,t}$ falling within this range, and use a range of lower values for real responses.

8.3.2 Simulation Parameters

Simulating the growth in each firms' declared gross profits, using a common trend, cycle and firm-specific components, yields a time profile of declared gross profits and deductions from which values of $\Omega'_{D,P*}$ and $\alpha = P^*/P^T$ can be obtained. In combination with assumed values for the autonomous elasticity components, these allow the overall behavioural elasticity, $\Omega_{PT,t}$ in (8.17), to be calculated for each period.

In producing simulations below, intermediate values from the range of empirical estimates discussed above are adopted for the benchmark autonomous elasticities: sensitivity to higher and lower values is examined in section 8.5. Table 8.2 shows that in the benchmark case, autonomous deductions shifting is assumed to be somewhat less, in absolute value, than profit-shifting, at 0.25 and -0.375 respectively. A relatively modest benchmark real response elasticity of -0.05 is assumed, reflecting a presumption that increasing or decreasing profits in a tax jurisdic-

tion via inter-jurisdictional mobility is likely to be easier than
generating net real increases in gross profit or deductions for the
firm. This is consistent with Clausing's (2009) US evidence, discussed above, that real responses are much smaller than profit-
shifting responses. These values are chosen not simply to reflect
multinational firms, but recognise that responses in aggregate
are affected by the mixture of domestic and multinational firms
existing in practice. Given fewer opportunities for profit shifting, the responses by domestic firms are likely to be lower than
those of most multinational firms.

Table 8.2: Benchmark Values for Aggregate Simulations

	Parameter	Benchmark	Comment
Profit shifting	$\Omega_{\theta_p,t}$	-0.375	
Deductions shifting	$\Omega_{\theta_d,t}$	0.25	
Real profit response	$\Omega_{P,t}$	-0.05	
Real deductions response	$\Omega'_{D,t}$	0.05	
Deduction-profit response	Ω_{D,P^*}	endogenous:	from CorpSim
Initial declared profit	P_0^*	exogenous:	
Initial declared deductions	D_0	endogenous:	from CorpSim
Trend profit growth		2%	
Profit growth cycle		0.4–3.6%	Range
(sine wave)		10	Wavelength

The effects of the asymmetric tax treatment of losses can
be expected to vary over the business cycle as changes in the
relative sizes of profits and losses affect deductions behaviour.
CorpSim was therefore run over a series of 10-period profit cycles described by a sine wave. In the benchmark simulation
this involves a trend growth rate of 2 per cent per period and
a low cycle (with growth in the range 0.4 to 3.6 per cent), with
trend growth observed in years 1, 6, 11, and so on. These profit
growth rates are well within the range of rates observed in the

UK in practice, with HMRC data showing annual growth rates for gross taxable profits as high as 18 per cent and as low as −4 per cent since the early 1990s. The benchmark also suppresses stochastics, so that the trend and cycle in profit growth rates affect all firms similarly.[7]

8.3.3 Profit Growth Cycles

Before examining elasticity results it is useful to consider the different growth cycles associated with different profit definitions. Previous sections have highlighted three profit definitions: gross profits, P; gross declared profits, P^*; and net taxable profits (after deductions), P^T. Official UK data measure only declared profits P^*, which can include losses, as with National Accounting definitions, or treat all losses as zero profits, as with HMRC gross taxable profit data. HMRC also measure net taxable profits, P^T, after losses and capital allowances have been used as offsets.

Figure 8.1 shows the exogenously set benchmark growth cycle for gross declared profits, including losses, dP^*/P^*, varying between 0.4 per cent and 3.6 per cent around the trend rate of 2 per cent. Gross profits liable to tax, where losses are set to zero, can be seen to follow a smoothed cycle compared with dP^*/P^*, ranging between 1.5 per cent and 2.5 per cent. For this benchmark case the effect of deductions is to generate a profile for net taxable profit growth which lies between the other two profiles – with slower deductions growth in above-trend years causing

---

[7]Nevertheless, the dynamic specification of the model implies that only firms with positive profits experience similar growth rates when there is no stochastic component of profit changes. For firms making large losses, growth rates are closer to the growth rate of the maximim possible loss. The precise relationship is given in Part III.

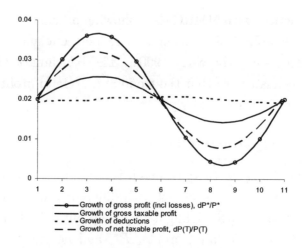

Figure 8.1: Profit Growth Rates Over the Cycle

net taxable profits to grow faster than the gross equivalent, and
vice versa in below-trend years. The deductions profile in Figure
8.1 does not display the same cyclical pattern as profits, due to
the opposing counter-cyclical and pro-cyclical effects of capital
allowances and losses used within the deductions total. Setting
capital allowances to zero, yields a regular counter-cyclical profile for deductions growth. The relationship between aggregate
gross (declared) and taxable profit growth is not straightforward.
It can be shown that:

$$\Omega_{P^T,P^*} = \sum_{i=1}^{N} \left(\eta_{P_i^T, P_i^*} \right) \left(\eta_{P_i^*, P^*} \right) \left(\frac{P_i^T}{P^T} \right) \qquad (8.18)$$

and therefore depends, among other things, on the way in which
individual firms' values of P_i^* varies with the aggregate P^*.

8.4 Benchmark Results

In estimating aggregate behavioural elasticities, CorpSim is used
to provide estimates of α for each firm, together with estimates
for profit growth and the resulting aggregate endogenous deductions elasticity, $\Omega_{D,P*}$. Together with assumed values for the behavioural responses in (8.17) this gives estimates of $\Omega_{PT,t}$. A useful comparison is with the case where declared deductions and
gross profits grow at the same rate: $\Omega_{D,P*} = 1$. This might be
expected to hold approximately during on-trend growth. Some
deviation from $\Omega_{D,P*} = 1$ during trend growth can arise because of tax law-induced lags in the claiming of losses as deductions and because, even in steady-state conditions, the extent
to which profits or deductions are declared at home could differ,
depending on the relative incentives and costs for each. Auerbach's (2007) evidence for the US, for example, seems to suggest
a long-term trend towards lower growth of tax loss deductions
than declared gross profits. Of particular interest among the
simulation results therefore is the sensitivity of $\Omega_{PT,t}$ to cyclical
changes, when $\Omega_{D,P*} \neq 1$.

Figure 8.2 shows elasticity profiles for $\Omega_{PT,t}$ over 11 periods
for two cases. In case A parameters are set at the benchmark
values in Table 8.2. In case B, $\Omega_{D,P*} = 1$ is imposed in all
periods. In both cases, α in (8.17) is allowed to vary over the
business cycle. The growth of dP^*/P^*, for the benchmark cycle
is also shown for comparison in Figure 8.2, on the right-hand
axis. The aggregate elasticities in Figure 8.2 are obtained from
simulations of 18,000 paired firms drawn from the initial simulated profit distributions described in the previous section. All
simulations reported follow an inital 20-year simulation period

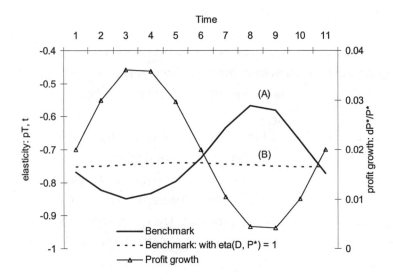

Figure 8.2: Elasticities Over the Cycle

which is necessary to prevent 'initial conditions' influencing the trend and cyclical components (for example, as loss pools build up from zero to trend levels).

First, it can be seen that the elasticity in profile B is approximately constant over the cycle, implying that the variation observed in profile A is almost entirely due to cyclical variations in Ω_{D,P^*}; that is, variations in α over the cycle have minimal effect. In these benchark cases α is around 2 on average across all firms. The trend value of $\Omega_{PT,t}$ is approximately -0.77. This can be seen using the benchmark parameters in Table 8.2 and equation (8.17), with $\alpha \approx 2$ and $\Omega_{D,P^*} \approx 1$ at mid-points in the cycle.

Comparing profiles A and B with the cycle in gross profit growth rates shows that during above-trend growth, the effect of differences in Ω_{D,P^*} are relatively small at the top of the cycle. The aggregate elasticity, $\Omega_{PT,t}$, reaches around -0.85 (or about 110 per cent of its trend value) in the benchmark case compared with -0.77 when $\Omega_{D,P^*} = 1$. This larger absolute value compared with the benchmark $\Omega_{PT,t}$ reflects the fact that $\Omega_{D,P^*} < 1$ during above-trend growth when there are fewer losses available. However, in recessionary years, when profit growth on average is low, $\Omega_{PT,t}$ in profile A deviates noticeably more from profile B, becoming -0.56, or around 73 per cent of its trend value, at the bottom of the cycle. This largely reflects the impact of especially large increases in Ω_{D,P^*} in association with cyclical downturns. The behaviour of η_{D,P^*} overall reflects the pro-cyclical charateristics of capital allowance deductions and the counter-cyclical characteristics of loss-based deductions. The latter tends to dominate.

The asymmetry between booms and recessions reflects the combined effect of the cyclical pattern of losses and their asymmetric treatment as deductions under the tax code. First, newly generated losses are larger in below-trend growth but smaller in above-trend growth. Second, because the taxable profit distribution is effectively truncated below zero, with restrictions imposed on the current and subsequent use of losses, this especially limits firms' ability to use their losses in recessions when positive profits are both smaller, and scarcer, on average. The asymmetry becomes more pronounced for larger profit cycles, as shown in Figure 8.3. The time profile for $\Omega_{PT,t}$ using a higher cycle (range: -0.05 per cent to 4.5 per cent around a 2 per cent trend) can be seen to be quite similar to the benchmark case during above-trend growth but substantially lower in absolute terms during below-trend growth.

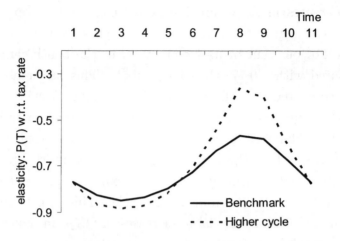

Figure 8.3: Elasticities with a High Profit Cycle

These results suggest an important conclusion for empirical methodologies testing for behavioural responses of profits or deductions to tax rate changes. Namely, in circumstances of trend or above-trend growth, recognising the impact of automatic changes in deductions may be less important. However, behavioural responses in recessionary periods could be substantially affected by the extent to which firms are constrained by the tying of deductions such as past losses to profits claimed in the home jurisdiction. In this context both the relative size of deductions and their endogenous relationship with profits are important.

8.5 Sensitivity Analyses

This section considers the effects on the cyclical pattern of the aggregate elasticity, $\eta_{PT,t}$, of varying a number of the parameters from their benchmark values. Subsection 8.5.1 examines the effects of different assumptions regarding profit and deductions shifting while subsection 8.5.2 discusses the role of stochastic changes in relative profit movements. Possible cyclical changes in the autonomous parameters are examined in subsection 8.5.3.

8.5.1 Alternative Shifting Assumptions

Figure 8.4 shows how the elasticity profiles change under different assumptions regarding the extent of shifting. The upper part of the figure considers different values of the profit-shifting elasticity, $\Omega_{\theta_p,t}$, while the lower part examines the effects of different deductions-shifting elasticities, $\Omega_{\theta_d,t}$. Other benchmark assumptions are maintained.

It can be seen that, for profit shifting, changing the values of the elasticity $\Omega_{\theta_p,t}$ causes the $\Omega_{PT,t}$ profiles to shift non-uniformly. At the depression part of the cycle, when absolute values of $\Omega_{PT,t}$ are relatively small, the shifting due to changed $\Omega_{\theta_p,t}$ values is small. The shift is larger when absolute values of $\Omega_{PT,t}$ are larger during boom periods. This reflects the fact that, since $\Omega_{\theta_p,t}$ is a component of $\Omega_{P^*,t}$, and is multiplied by Ω_{D,P^*} in (8.17), this magifies the impact on the tax base elasticity, $\Omega_{PT,t}$. However, for deductions shifting there is no such multiplier effect via Ω_{D,P^*} and therefore the profiles shift uniformly when $\Omega_{\theta_d,t}$ is changed, regardless of the point in the cycle.

In general, benchmark or lower response assumptions (for ex-

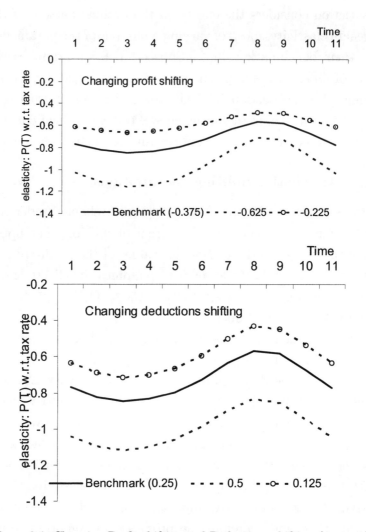

Figure 8.4: Changing Profit-shifting and Deductions-shifting Assumptions

ample, $\Omega_{\theta_p,t} = -0.225$; $\Omega_{\theta_d,t} = 0.125$) yield values for $\Omega_{PT,t}$ which are smaller than -0.8. However, the higher response assumptions (for example, $\Omega_{\theta_p,t} = -0.625$; $\Omega_{\theta_d,t} = 0.5$) can yield values of $\Omega_{PT,t}$ in excess of -1. In view of the relationship in equation (8.9), this implies a negative tax elasticity, $\Omega_{T,t} < 0$, which in turn implies that tax rates are set on the negatively sloped portion of the corporate tax Laffer curve. Such elasticity values seem unlikely to hold for the current UK tax regime, though they are consitent with some of the international estimates reported above. This finding therefore suggests either that the lower behavioural responses examined are more likely in practice, or when automatic effects raise the value of $\Omega_{PT,t}$, *ceteris paribus*, this may induce changes in firms' discretionary responses, $\eta_{\theta_p,t}$, $\eta_{P,t}$, and so on. In either case, the contribution of endogenous deduction responses to $\Omega_{PT,t}$ appears to be quite large when compared with the contribution of 'autonomous' components. Subsection 8.5.3 considers possible trade-offs between automatic and autonomous responses.

8.5.2 Allowing for Stochastic Profit Growth

So far it has been assumed that all firms making positive gross profits grow at the same rate. To capture the possibility of a range of firm profit growth rates, CorpSim incorporates a random growth component. Simulations reported below use a variance of profit growth of 0.0001 around mean growth as determind by the trend and cycle components. This implies, for example, that with 2 per cent trend growth on average, around half of all firms experience profit growth outside a 1 to 3 per cent range. This has the effect of generating an additional source of difference in $\eta_{D,P*}$ across firms, with resulting differences in the aggregate equivalent $\Omega_{D,P*}$.

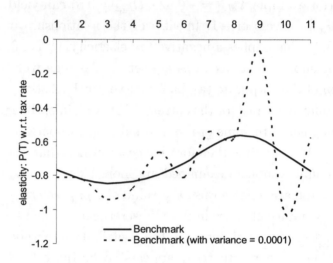

Figure 8.5: Allowing for Stochastic Component in Profit Growth

The resulting time profile for $\Omega_{P^T,t}$ is shown in Figure 8.5 where it is compared with the zero variance benchmark case. It can be seen that elasticity values can vary quite considerably especially, but not exclusively, associated with the cyclical downturn during years 6 to 11, when negative profit growth is more prevalent. The previous chapter showed that the built-in flexibility of corporation tax (the aggregate elasticity of tax revenue with respect to aggregate profits) is also inherently variable over the business cycle, and this variability increases when stochastic elements are introduced. The results suggest that automatic responses of deductions to changes in profits declared at home can be quite volatile. Thus, individual firms' choices to shift profits abroad may be quite different, depending on the size and growth of their deductions, since these can only be claimed against profits declared at home. The simulations suggest that these factors may be important at the aggregate level. This is perhaps not surprising when it is recalled that the vast bulk of corporate tax revenues in the UK are paid by a small fraction of large taxpaying firms. For example, in 2003–04, the largest 7 per cent of corporate taxpayers contributed 87 per cent of total corporation tax revenues. Volatility in their profit performances could have a large influence on aggregate taxable profit outcomes.

8.5.3 Cyclical Changes in Responses

The results reported so far are based on an assumption that the four aggregate autonomous elasticities that reflect firms' choices independent of profit levels ($\Omega_{\theta_p,t}$, $\Omega_{P,t}$, $\Omega_{\theta_d,t}$, $\Omega'_{D,t}$) remain unchanged in the face of profit-induced changes in firms' abilities to claim deductions. Clearly, when recessionary forces reduce firms' deductions claiming (or increase the required profits declared at home to use those deductions), they may be expected to react. In particular, they may seek to mitigate endogenous effects by increasing or reducing any of the relevant behavioural elasticities.

This could be investigated in the current context by specifying a relationship between automatic and discretionary responses. However, in the absense of empirical evidence on the nature and extent of firms' behavioural responses, such modelled relationships would be arbitrary. As an alternative, this subsection considers the changes in each behavioural response that would be required to keep the tax base elasticity, $\Omega_{P^T,t}$ constant, given the automatic changes induced by cyclical factors;

that is, if discretionary behavioural changes aimed to neutralise fully the endogenous changes.

Rearranging equation (8.17) and letting $\lambda = \alpha - (\alpha - 1)\Omega_{D,P^*}$, the two discretionary elasticities, $\Omega_{P^*,t}$ and $\Omega_{D,t}$, can be expressed as:

$$\Omega_{P^*,t} = \frac{1}{\lambda}\left\{(\alpha - 1)\Omega_{D,t} + \Omega_{PT,t}\right\} \qquad (8.19)$$

and

$$\Omega_{D,t} = \frac{1}{(\alpha - 1)}\left\{\lambda\Omega_{P^*,t} - \Omega_{PT,t}\right\} \qquad (8.20)$$

where, in each case, the elasticities on the right hand side are held constant at their benchmark values. Changes in the left-hand-side elasticities are then determined by variations in α and Ω_{D,P^*}.

Results are reported in Table 8.3 for a complete cycle. These examples use the period 1 benchmark tax base elasticity of $\Omega_{PT,t} = -0.77$, as shown in Figure 8.2, yielding the benchmark behavioural elasticities $\Omega_{P^*,t} = -0.43$ and $\Omega_{D,t} = 0.30$ in period 1, in which the endogenous response, $\Omega_{D,P^*} \approx 1$. That is $\Omega_{P^*,t} = -(0.375 + 0.05)$, and $\Omega_{D,t} = 0.25 + 0.05$. The two columns of Table 8.3 show the values of the discretionary total profit or deductions responses, using (8.19) and (8.20) respectively, which maintain $\Omega_{PT,t} = -0.77$. It can be seen in column 1, for example, that if $\Omega_{P^*,t}$ is adjusted to compensate fully for cyclical effects, this has to rise (in absolute terms) from -0.43 in period 1 to -0.78 at the cyclical low point in period 8. That is, combined real and shifting profit responses would need to increase by around 80 per cent. To put this in perspective, recall that a profit response of -0.43 implies that a 10 per cent increase in the tax rate would cause declared profits, on average, to fall from, say, 80 to 77. The value of -0.78 implies a fall from 80 to around 74. Column 2 shows that the equivalent response for deductions involves a deductions elasticity, $\Omega_{D,t}$, in period 8 more than 60 per cent higher than its value when growth is on-trend in period 1, increasing from 0.30 to 0.49.

Table 8.3: Compensatory Shifting and Real Responses

Year	Total profit response $\Omega_{P*,t}$	Total deductions response $\Omega_{D,t}$
1	−0.43	0.30
2	−0.38	0.25
3	−0.36	0.23
4	−0.37	0.24
5	−0.40	0.28
6	−0.47	0.34
7	−0.61	0.43
8	−0.78	0.49
9	−0.73	0.48
10	−0.57	0.39
11	−0.43	0.30

The changes in the profit and deductions responses in Table 8.3 are shown in Figure 8.6, as precentages of trend values (period 1). This shows that both the required profit and deduction responses (needed to keep the overall behavioural response, $\Omega_{PT,t}$, constant) are larger in recessions, reflecting the fact that the positive indirect effect from $\Omega_{D,P*}$ is greater in recessions and hence needs a larger discretionary reponse to counteract it. Figure 8.6 also shows however that the required change in the profit response is less than that for deductions in above-trend growth, and vice versa in below-trend growth. This arises because the indirect effect $\Omega_{D,P*}$, operating through $\Omega_{P*,t}$, is less than unity in above-trend growth but is greater than unity in below-trend growth. Thus the effect on the profit response is re-

spectively dampened then magnified, over the cycle, compared
with the deductions response.

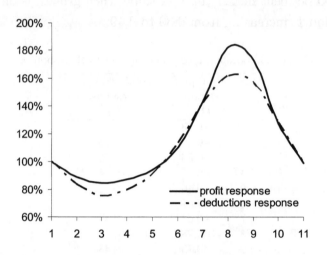

Figure 8.6: Percentage Profit and Deductions Responses

It is perhaps not surprising that, when recessions restrict a
firm's ability to shift profits out (due to the greater simultane-
ous loss of automatic deductions at home), more discretionary
deductions should be shifted into the home jurisdiction. That
declared profits should be reduced even more in this situation is
less clear. However, this result follows from the condition that
$\Omega_{D,P^*} < \alpha/(\alpha - 1)$. Since this condition holds here, reducing
declared profits reduces automatic deductions claiming but by
less than the reduction in profits. Hence, reducing declared gross
profits also reduces declared net profits, despite the loss of some
automatic deductions. In a recession, shifting profits out (which
reduces tax liability) simultaneously shifts a greater amount of
deductions (which increases tax liability) compared with non-

recessionary periods. Hence more profits must be shifted ($\Omega_{P*,t}$ must be higher) in order to stop tax liability rising, and keep the overall response, $\Omega_{PT,t}$, constant. Nevertheless, Table 8.3 and Figure 8.6 show that, in a recession, a given overall behavioural response can be achieved via a smaller change in the deductions response compared with the profit response.

8.6 Conclusions

This aim of this chapter has been to examine behavioural responses by companies to changes in the taxation of their profits in the home country, and the impact on this of the asymmetric tax treatment of losses. Emphasis has been on the elasticity of net or taxable profits with respect to a change in the tax rate. This elasticity can take the form of real responses, where activities are transferred to other tax jurisdictions, and income-shifting responses in which the location of economic activity is unchanged but the extent to which profits and deductions are declared in the home country changes. This chapter has shown that it is also important to distinguish separate responses of gross profits and of deductions allowable as profit offsets. Where, as in the UK, these deductions are relatively large and are related to the size of companies' profits, it was found that allowing for an endogenous, or automatic, response may be important for empirical estimates of firms' overall behavioural responses.

A decomposition of behavioural responses to tax changes was used to identify the contribution of both autonomous and endogenous deductions responses. The elasticity of taxable profits with respect to the tax rate was shown to depend on, among other things, the endogenous elasticity of deductions with respect to declared profits. Using a microsimulation model based on profit and deductions data for the UK, this endogenous or automatic response of deductions to profit changes was shown to play an important role.

The elasticity of aggregate taxable profits with respect to the tax rate, $\Omega_{PT,t}$, was found to be pro-cyclical, being in absolute terms at a maximum when aggregate profit growth is at a maximum, and an absolute minimum in the depths of the depression part of the business cycle. Importantly, the variation in the $\Omega_{PT,t}$ was found to be almost entirely due to cyclical variations in the endogenous elasticity mentioned above, rather than variations in the *size* of deductions relative to gross profits over the cycle. This endogenous component was also found to be substantial compared with typical empirical estimates of profit-shifting responses which ignore such endogeneity. However, the relative size of deductions is important in so far as this affects whether the condition $\eta_{D,P*} < \alpha/(\alpha - 1)$ is met; that is whether endogenous deduction responses tend to raise or lower tax liabilities when declared profits change.

However, the variation in $\Omega_{PT,t}$ was not symmetric, being greater in periods of recession. This asymmetry between booms and recessions arises both because losses are relatively more important in below-trend growth, and because their asymmetric treatment in the tax code is most pronounced in such periods. This cyclical asymmetry was found to increase as the amplitude of the profit cycle increases, and allowing for a stochastic element to firms' profit growth produced a more volatile taxable profit elasticity due to the greater volatility in deductions used by firms.

The implication of these findings for empirical attempts to

measure behavioural responses of profits or deductions to tax rate changes is that in circumstances of trend or above-trend growth, recognising the impact of automatic changes in deductions may be relatively less important. However, behavioural responses in recessions could be substantially affected by the extent to which firms are constrained by the tying of deductions such as past losses to profits claimed in the home jurisdiction.

These results are consistent with Auerbach's (2007) conclusion, for the US, that evidence of a declining use of tax losses by companies in aggregate questions the importance of profit-shifting. They also point to a need for empirical estimates of profit responses to tax rate changes to recognise the potential for effects arising from automatic changes in deductions in association with changes in declared profits.

Part V

Conclusions

Chapter 9

Conclusions

This book began by stressing that the growth in aggregate corporation tax revenues in relation to that of profits, or GDP, is highly volatile from year to year. The volatility has serious implications for attempts to forecast corporation tax revenue, which are among the most difficult to forecast using conventional methods, based on regressions of taxes and profits over time. Such regressions may be able to approximate the long-run buoyancy of corporation taxes. But they are limited in their ability to deal with cyclical aspects and cannot capture discretionary tax changes. A major argument of this book is that the volatility of corporation tax revenue is an inherent feature of the system. In examining the potential changes in revenue, it is suggested that a microsimulation model can be a valuable tool of analysis.

While microsimulation has been successfully applied in the context of the personal tax and transfer system, using databases from widely available household surveys, there is very little experience of such models to examine corporation taxes. A severe constraint arises from the scarcity of appropriate data. Furthermore, corporation taxes are highly complex, partly because of the dynamic role played by losses and their asymmetric treatment, and because of the ability of corporations to form groups for tax purposes, thereby allowing the sharing of losses to some extent. In addition corporations typically obtain income from various sources, which are treated differently by the tax system. This book reports an attempt to construct and use such a model, called CorpSim. Inevitably the model involves many simplifications, but it is capable of capturing many features of corporation taxes and their variability which are observed in practice. In view of the data limitations, any results must of course be regarded as tentative.

In contructing household microsimulation models, recent developments have enabled researchers to allow for potential labour supply effects of tax and transfer changes (though many models continue to be restricted to the analysis of 'impact effects' of tax changes). Nevertheless, there are many possible behavioural responses – such as household formation, fertility, retirement behaviour and geographical mobility – which present challenges for future work. In constructing a corporation tax model, the modelling of behaviour must inevitably be limited. One important aspect involves the role of various allowances and the use of losses. Another involves the use of income shifting from one country to another. In the first case, extensive algorithms were developed in order to compute the tax minimising configuration of declarations over time. In the second case, a more limited approach was taken whereby an attempt was made to throw some light on such shifting by decomposing the likely responses to tax changes into a variety of components, some of which can be measured using the microsimulation model.

Part II of this book was concerned with the major concepts

and theoretical issues. In examining tax changes, the focus of attention was on the concept of the tax revenue elasticity, defined as the proportional change in revenue divided by the proportional change in profits, for an unchanged tax regime. This concept is central to analyses of 'fiscal drag'. Chapter 2 examined the conceptual issues involved in assessing the corporation tax revenue elasticity. It was shown that deductions, and how they change as profits grow, play a crucial role in determining whether corporation tax revenues are expected to grow faster or slower than profits. For small firms, the nature of the corporate tax schedule – the tax rates and thresholds applied to net profits – can be important for their revenue elasticities.

Considerable attention was given to the important role of cyclical factors, and consideration of the circumstances in which the corporation tax revenue elasticity deviates from its expected long-run value of 1, when tax and profits grow at the same rate. The volatility of the corporation tax revenue elasticity suggests that much of the observed volatility in corporation tax receipts and accruals could indeed be an inherent property of the corporation tax system, given the volatility in the tax base, profits. In mild economic downturns, corporation tax revenue elasticities may rise (because tax growth falls less than profit growth), but in more severe downturns, large but temporary increases and decreases in the revenue elasticity – and even negative elasticities – can be expected.

Chapter 3 turned to the treatment of losses, which is less generous than positive profits in the corporate tax codes of many countries. In present value terms, losses generate a lower tax rebate than the positive tax levied on equivalent sized positive profits. This asymmetry has two opposing effects on corporate tax liabilities when corporate losses increase. On the one hand increased losses give rise to a larger 'base' for tax rebates. On the other hand, the asymmetries of the tax code bind more tightly when losses are larger, which has the effect of pushing up the effective average tax rate. Chapter 3 considered the relevance of this phenomenon for estimates of companies' behavioural responses to changes in corporate tax rates. These responses involve shifting profits and losses into or out of the tax jurisdiction.

In order to make the effective tax rate applied to losses more transparent, an equivalent tax function facing a firm was specified having the same present value of tax revenue as the actual function but allowing for a (partial) rebate in each period, where appropriate. This function involved a measure of asymmetry equal to the present value of the period's losses as tax offsets, as a ratio of their nominal value. It was shown that asymmetries in the way losses are treated reduce tax revenue responses to tax rate changes. The size of this reduction increases as the asymmetry increases. This effect was found to be nonlinear with respect to the economic cycle, being disproportionately strong during recessions (when losses are relatively large) but disproportionately weak during booms (when losses are small). These disproportionate effects of recessions are larger the smaller is the asymmetry. Behavioural responses of tax revenue to tax rate changes are thus likely to be smaller for tax regimes which impose greater constraints on loss use within the tax code and when these responses are measured during periods when corporate losses are abnormally high. However, when losses are abnormally low, larger behavioural responses are likely to be observed.

Chapter 4 turned to an examination of the composition of behavioural responses to changes in profits taxation in the home country, and the possible pattern of such responses over the business cycle. Emphasis was on the determinants of the elasticity of corporation tax paid, by individual firms and in aggregate, in response to a change in the corporation tax rate. This elasticity is closely related to the elasticity of net or taxable profits with respect to a change in the tax rate. Responses to tax rate changes can take the form of real responses, in which real activities change or are relocated to other tax jurisdictions, and income-shifting responses in which the location of economic activity is unchanged but the extent to which incomes are declared in the home country changes. This chapter showed that it is also important to distinguish separate responses of gross profits and of deductions allowable as profit offsets. In particular, the overall elasticity of taxable profits with respect to the tax rate can be decomposed into four elasticities relating to real/shifting and profit/deduction responses, along with the ratio of gross declared profits to taxable profits. The size and type of 'qualifying expenditures' was shown to be important as this determines both the extent of deductions and their endogenous or automatic adjustment in association with profit changes. This endogenous response directly impacts on measures of overall tax responsiveness.

The endogenous deductions response can be summarised by the elasticity of aggregate taxable profits with respect to gross declared profits. This was found to be pro-cyclical, leading to a counter-cyclical variation in the elasticity of total revenue with respect to the tax rate. However, this variation is unlikely to be symmetric, being especially pronounced in periods of recession. This asymmetry between booms and recessions arises because

of the asymmetric treatment of losses in the tax code, together
with the fact that losses tend to be relatively unimportant as tax
deductions in circumstances of trend, or above-trend, growth.
The asymmetry increases as the amplitude of the profit cycle
increases.

These findings have implications for empirical attempts to
measure behavioural responses of tax revenue or profits to corporate tax rate changes. The nature and extent of corporate
tax deductions, especially losses, can be expected to give rise to
quite different behavioural response estimates. This is especially
true for countries where tax codes display greater asymmetry
in their treatment of losses, and in relatively high loss (recession) circumstances. In this context, firms are likely to be more
constrained by the endogenous 'tying' of deductions to profits
claimed in their home jurisdiction. By contrast, even with asymmetric loss treatment, estimates of responses may be relatively
unaffected when firms' profits are above-trend.

Part III presented the basic structure of the microsimulation
model, CorpSim. Chapter 5 described a model of the distribution and dynamics of UK corporate profits. The aim was to
construct a model that is capable of providing the basis of a
corporate tax microsimulation model which can generate profits
over a number of years. This requirement differs from that of
household models, where one cross-sectional dataset is sufficient.
Although many simplifications were required in constructing and
calibrating the model, it is able to capture many of the crucial
features of the distribution of profits in the UK and their relative
movements.

Chapter 6 completed the model description by outlining algorithms for determining the use of capital allowances and losses as

deductions, in the case of single firms and of firms within groups. The latter case is considerably more complex, even with just two firms within a group. In some cases a numerical search procedure is required. However, this extra complexity was found to be worthwhile, compared with a more mechanical approach, as it is able to approximate much more closely a net profit minimising, and thus tax minimising, strategy.

Part IV makes use of the microsimulation model to examine several feature of corporation tax revenue over the business cycle. Chapter 7 considered how corporation tax receipts are expected to grow over time, given an unchanged corporation tax regime and compliance effort. This is important for two reasons. First, with growing public expenditure demands, it is necessary for tax authorities to know whether, in the absence of budgetary changes, they can expect improving or worsening revenues from corporation tax both over the longer term and within an economic cycle. Second, if corporation tax revenues can rise or fall without any changes in compliance, but revenue targets are used to assess compliance effort, the ability to meet these will be influenced by factors inherent to the corporation tax system but outside the control of compliance units.

The growth of aggregate corporation tax revenue appears to be highly volatile in relation to the growth of profits. Volatility in revenue elasticities is generally less when groups can share losses compared with an economy composed only of single firms. Relatively high volatility in revenue elasticities is especially associated with economic downturns, otherwise elasticities tend to hover around a value of 1. This volatility occurs even when all firms' profits are assumed to grow at the same rate, but is exacerbated when random factors allow some firms to deviate from this common growth rate. In mild economic downturns, corporation tax revenue elasticities may rise, because tax growth falls less than profit growth, but in more severe downturns, large but temporary decreases in the revenue elasticity, and even negative elasticities, can be expected. Capital allowances and losses claimed against positive profits were found to have quite different effects on revenue elasticities, if in general capital allowances are positively correlated (and losses negatively correlated) with profits.

The simulations model focused on how revenues change relative to the tax base, suggesting that these are expected to be quite unstable in the short run. How the tax base, profits, might change over time requires a separate analysis recognising behavioural factors, including the potential for the tax regime itself to influence firms' profitability and how and where their profits are declared for tax purposes. Chapter 8 turned to examine behavioural responses by companies to changes in the taxation of their profits in the home country, and the impact on this of the asymmetric tax treatment of losses. Here use was made of analytical results produced in Part II, and emphasis was on the elasticity of net or taxable profits with respect to a change in the tax rate. Chapter 8 showed, as first suggested in chapter 4, that it is also important to distinguish separate responses of gross profits and of deductions allowable as profit offsets. The elasticity of taxable profits with respect to the tax rate was shown to depend on, among other things, the endogenous elasticity of deductions with respect to declared profits. Where, as in the UK, these deductions are relatively large and are related to the size of companies' profits, it was found that allowing for an endogenous, or automatic, response may be important for empirical estimates of firms' overall behavioural responses.

The elasticity of aggregate taxable profits with respect to the tax rate was found to be pro-cyclical, being in absolute terms at a maximum when aggregate profit growth is at a maximum, and an absolute minimum in the depths of the depression part of the business cycle. Importantly, the variation was found to be almost entirely due to cyclical variations in the endogenous elasticity mentioned above, rather than variations in the size of deductions relative to gross profits over the cycle. This endogenous component was also found to be substantial compared with typical empirical estimates of profit-shifting responses which ignore such endogeneity. The variation was not symmetric, being greater in periods of recession. This asymmetry between booms and recessions arises both because losses are relatively more important in below-trend growth, and because their asymmetric treatment in the tax code is most pronounced in such periods. This cyclical asymmetry was found to increase as the amplitude of the profit cycle increases, and allowing for a stochastic element to firms' profit growth produced a more volatile taxable profit elasticity due to the greater volatility in deductions used by firms.

This book has therefore explored a relatively new approach to examining corporation taxation and its variation over time, involving the specification and construction of a dynamic microsimulation model for the UK. This represents a substantial challenge in view of the paucity of suitable data and the complexity of corporation taxation compared, for example, with personal income taxation, along with the need to consider multiple income sources, firms within groups and the associated complexities of the use of losses over time. While simulation results must inevitably be treated with caution, the analysis has suggested that the observed variability in profits taxation may well be an inherent feature of the tax structure. Recent events have indeed confirmed the considerable sensitivity of revenue in the face of strong recessions. Improvements in the modelling of profit dynamics with multiple sources, and the changes in behaviour resulting from tax rate and structure changes, present serious challenges for future research. Progress will clearly depend to some extent on wider access to suitable data, just as progress in household microsimulation models required access to confidentialised unit record data.

Appendix A

Tax Loss Deductions When Future Tax Rates Vary

The analysis of tax loss asymmetries in chapter 3 assumed that expected tax rates do not change. That is, following a one-off change to the corporate tax rate, firm's responses are based on a presumption that this rate remains constant into the future. This assumption is readily altered by redefining the loss 'deductions rate', s_j, to allow for variable future tax rates. In defining the tax function, s_j was defined as the present value at j of period j's losses as tax offsets, as a proportion of their nominal value, L_j, over the period $k = 0, ..., K$. The present value of the tax liability associated with these losses is, from (3.5), simply $ts_j L_j$. Instead, defining t_k as the tax rate applicable in period k (and $t_j = t_0$), $s_{j,k}$ can be defined as:

$$s_{j,k} = \sum_{k=0}^{K} \frac{t_k q_{j,k}}{(1+r)^k} \qquad \text{(A.1)}$$

The term $ts_j L_j$ is thus replaced by $s_{j,k} L_j$. Equation (A.1) captures the fact that the future tax deduction value of current, unclaimed losses depends on the future tax rate applicable when these losses are used as tax offsets, compared with the tax rate applicable if these losses were used concurrently.

Incorporating variable future tax rates into the responses in equations (3.18) and (3.19) is less straightforward. The key response examined, $\eta_{\theta_j,t}$, becomes η_{θ_j,t_j}. But the response of the current net profit ratio, θ_j, to changes in t_k would also need to be considered, if responses were conditioned both by the immediate change in the tax rate and expected future changes in tax rates. In addition, actual or expected changes in t_k may be a function of changes in t_j if, for example, a cut in the corporate tax rate were to make it less likely that the rate will be cut in future years.

Appendix B

Calculating Net Profits: Single Firms

This appendix summarises how net taxable profits are derived from gross taxable profits in the simulation model for the case of a single firm (that is, one that is not a member of a group). Given two profit sources, there are four possible combinations of profit/loss for such firms: both sources in profit, either source in loss, and both sources in loss.

Both Profit Sources are Positive

Consider the first case shown in Table 6.2, where P_t^A and P_t^B are both positive. First, capital allowances are deducted against P_t^A where possible, giving profit net of capital allowances claimed, NCP_t^A, as:

$$NCP_t^A = \max\left(0, P_t^A - CA_t^A\right) \tag{B.1}$$

with capital allowances claimed, CAC_t^A, equal to:

$$CAC_t^A = \min\left(P_t^A, CA_t^A\right) \tag{B.2}$$

After dealing with source A, any excess capital allowances, XCA_t^A, are treated as equivalent to A losses which can either be carried forward to the next period or offset against source B profits currently. The amount available for claiming against source B is thus:

$$XCA_t^A = \max\left(0, CA_t^A - CAC_t^A\right) \tag{B.3}$$

Assuming, as above, a preference to first use excess capital allowances to offset B profits, then B profits net of capital allowance are:

$$NCP_t^B = \max\left(0, P_t^B - XCA_t^A\right) \tag{B.4}$$

and the amount of XCA_t actually claimed, CAC_t^B, is:

$$CAC_t^B = \min\left(P_t^B, XCA_t^A\right) \tag{B.5}$$

Let NP_t^A denote profits net of all deductions. In this case, these are capital allowances and losses brought forward and claimed. Further, let LC_t^A denote losses claimed in relation to source A, with similar notation for source B. Thus, losses brought forward are deducted from net-of-capital-allowance profits to give net profits:

$$NP_t^A = \max\left(0, NCP_t^A - LP_{t-1}^A\right) \tag{B.6}$$

with A losses claimed:

$$LC_t^A = \min\left(NCP_t^A, LP_{t-1}^A\right) \tag{B.7}$$

and

$$NP_t^B = \max\left(0, NCP_t^B - LP_{t-1}^B\right) \tag{B.8}$$

with B losses claimed:

$$LC_t^B = \min\left(NCP_t^B, LP_{t-1}^B\right) \tag{B.9}$$

The resulting loss pools, LP_t^A and LP_t^B, to be carried forward to the next period are simply given by last year's loss pool plus any additional losses incurred during t (from excess capital allowances in this case), less losses and excess capital allowances claimed at t. Thus:

$$LP_t^A = LP_{t-1}^A - LC_t^A + XCA_t^A - CAC_t^B \qquad \text{(B.10)}$$

and:

$$LP_t^B = LP_{t-1}^B - LC_t^B \qquad \text{(B.11)}$$

The firm's corporation tax liability can be calculated by applying the corporation tax rates/thresholds to total net taxable profits, P_t^T, of:

$$P_t^T = NP_t^A + NP_t^B \qquad \text{(B.12)}$$

Finally, in this and the three following cases, capital allowances available, CA_t^A, are given by equation (6.3) in Subsection 3.1.1. Similarly, the capital allowance pool available at the end of period t in each case is:

$$CP_t^A = (1 - \delta) \left\{ CP_{t-1}^A + I_t \right\} \qquad \text{(B.13)}$$

Positive Profit in A and Loss in B

Where P_t^A is positive and P_t^B is negative, a B loss is defined as $L_t^B = -P_t^B$. Capital allowances are again claimed first so that profit net of capital allowances claimed, NCP_t^A, is given by:

$$NCP_t^A = \max \left(0, P_t^A - CA_t^A \right) \qquad \text{(B.14)}$$

with capital allowances claimed, CAC_t^A, equal to:

$$CAC_t^A = \min \left(P_t^A, CA_t^A \right) \qquad \text{(B.15)}$$

After dealing with source A, any excess capital allowances (to be added to the A loss pool) are again given by:

$$XCA_t^A = \max\left(0, CA_t^A - CAC_t^A\right) \qquad (B.16)$$

Next, current losses in B are used to offset any remaining profits in A. Let $NL^B P_t^A$ denote profits net of capital allowances and B losses, claimed against A profits, and let LC_t^B denote B losses claimed in period t. Thus:

$$NL^B P_t^A = \max\left(0, NCP_t^A - L_t^B\right) \qquad (B.17)$$

$$LC_t^B = \min\left(NCP_t^A, L_t^B\right) \qquad (B.18)$$

Finally, previous losses in A, brought forward, are used to offset any remaining profits in A. Hence:

$$NP_t^A = \max\left(0, NL^B P_t^A - LP_{t-1}^A\right) \qquad (B.19)$$

with $NP_t^B = 0$.

Finally A losses claimed are:

$$LC_t^A = \min\left(NL^B P_t^A, LP_{t-1}^A\right) \qquad (B.20)$$

which affects the loss pools, LP_t^A and LP_t^B, given by:

$$LP_t^A = LP_{t-1}^A - LC_t^A + XCA_t^A \qquad (B.21)$$

and:

$$LP_t^B = LP_{t-1}^B - LC_t^B + L_t^B \qquad (B.22)$$

Positive Profit in B and Loss in A

Suppose that P_t^B is positive and P_t^A is negative, with $L_t^A = -P_t^A$. In the absence of profits in A, capital allowances are first offset against profit in B, in the form of excess capital allowances, XCA_t^A. Profits in B net of capital allowances claimed, NCP_t^B, are given by:

$$NCP_t^B = \max\left(0, P_t^B - XCA_t^A\right) \qquad (B.23)$$

with capital allowances claimed, CAC_t^B, equal to:

$$CAC_t^B = \min\left(P_t^B, XCA_t^A\right) \qquad (B.24)$$

Next, losses in A are used to offset any remaining profits in B. Let $NL^A P_t^B$ denote B profits net of capital allowances and current A losses claimed, and let LC_t^A denote those A loss claims. Thus:

$$NL^A P_t^B = \max\left(0, NCP_t^B - L_t^A\right) \qquad (B.25)$$

and

$$LC_t^A = \min\left(NCP_t^B, L_t^A\right) \qquad (B.26)$$

Finally, previous losses in B that were carried forward are used to offset any remaining profits in B. Hence, losses from source B claimed against source B profit are:

$$LC_t^B = \min(NL^A P_t^B, LP_{t-1}^B) \qquad (B.27)$$

and net profits are given by:

$$NP_t^B = \max\left(0, NL^A P_t^B - LP_{t-1}^B\right) \qquad (B.28)$$

$$NP_t^A = 0. \qquad (B.29)$$

The loss pools, LP_t^A and LP_t^B, are given by:

$$LP_t^A = LP_{t-1}^A + L_t^A - LC_t^A + XCA_t^A - CAC_t^B \qquad (B.30)$$

and:

$$LP_t^B = LP_{t-1}^B - LC_t^B \qquad (B.31)$$

Losses in Both A and B

The case where losses arise from both sources is simple, as all losses and capital allowances are carried forward. When both P_t^A and P_t^B are negative, then $L_t^A = -P_t^A$ and $L_t^B = -P_t^B$ and $NP_t^A = NP_t^B = 0$. Current A losses and capital allowances are added to the A loss pool to be carried forward, and current B losses are added to the B loss pool.

Appendix C

Empirical Analysis of Mobility

This Appendix uses UK profits data, for each source considered separately, to examine a simple dynamic process involving changes in $x = P + d$ over time. To abstract, for the time being, from changes in the geometric mean income, define for the ith firm, $z_{it} = \log(x_{it}) - \mu_t$, where μ_t is the mean of logarithms of the overall distribution of x. The same process is assumed to apply over the complete distribution, so components of the mixture distributions discussed above are ignored here. A simple Markov process is described by:

$$z_{it} = z_{it-1} + u_{it} \tag{C.1}$$

where the u_{it} are independently normally distributed. Allowing a tendency for those in the higher ranges of the distribution to obtain proportionately smaller increases than those in the lower deciles involves subtracting the term $(1 - \beta)\, z_{it-1}$ from the right-hand side of (C.1). Thus when firm i's profits at $t - 1$ are below the geometric mean, the logarithm of relative earnings, z_{it-1}, is negative. This means that the average change is greater than that of the geometric mean, so long as $\beta < 1$. This gives 'regression towards the mean' as:

$$z_{it} = \beta z_{it-1} + u_{it} \qquad (C.2)$$

If there is a tendency for improvements to depend to some extent on previous success, a first-order auto-regressive process for the u_{it} applies, such that:

$$u_{it} = \gamma u_{i,t-1} + \varepsilon_{it} \qquad (C.3)$$

where γ is assumed to be the same for all firms, and ε_{it} is distributed independently of previous values with variance σ_ε^2. Combining this with (C.2), and eliminating the u's from each, gives:

$$z_{it} = (\gamma + \beta) z_{it-1} - \gamma\beta z_{it-2} + \varepsilon_{it} \qquad (C.4)$$

Hence a firm's relative profit depends on its value in the previous two years. Examination of this type of process therefore requires information about individuals' incomes in three successive years.

To estimate the parameters β, γ and σ_ε^2 of the mobility process, using data for three consecutive years, rewrite equation (C.4) as:

$$z_{it} = a z_{it-1} + b z_{it-2} + \varepsilon_{it} \qquad (C.5)$$

where $a = \gamma + \beta$ and $b = -\gamma\beta$. The parameters of equation (C.5) can be estimated using ordinary least squares, though in practice $\log(x_{it})$ can be used instead of z_{it}, giving a constant term in the regression equation. However, there is an identification problem because of the lack of exogenous variables. From the two above equations relating γ and β to a and b, it is required to express β and γ as functions of the coefficients a and b. Using $\gamma = -b/\beta$ and substituting in $a = \gamma + \beta$ gives the following quadratic in β:

$$\beta^2 - a\beta - b = 0 \qquad (C.6)$$

Using the two equations to solve for γ gives a quadratic of precisely the same form. An approach is to impose an *a priori* condition that β is close to unity, so the larger root of the quadratic (C.6) is taken as its estimate; the smaller root is taken as the estimate of γ. Hence the estimates are:

$$\beta = 0.5 \left[a + \left(a^2 + 4b \right)^{0.5} \right] \tag{C.7}$$

$$\gamma = 0.5 \left[a - \left(a^2 + 4b \right)^{0.5} \right] \tag{C.8}$$

where a, b, β and γ are understood to be estimates, although for convenience 'hats' have been omitted.

Estimates, using the profit data for sources A and B, are reported in Table C.1, for each of the imposed values of d. The standard errors are in all cases virtually zero, given the large size of the samples used (shown in the final column of the table). These results suggest that there is some regression towards the mean and some negative serial correlation, with lower values of each term for source B compared with A (that is, more regression and less serial correlation).

Table C.1: Profit Regressions

d	Constant	a	b	R^2	β	γ	N
Profit source A							
400	0.51	0.6562	0.2627	0.773	0.937	-0.280	26315
500	0.60	0.6486	0.2595	0.758	0.928	-0.280	26716
600	0.64	0.6465	0.2578	0.761	0.925	-0.279	27047
700	0.68	0.6701	0.2309	0.745	0.921	-0.251	27330
800	0.74	0.6541	0.2399	0.743	0.916	-0.262	27580
900	0.75	0.6581	0.2356	0.736	0.915	-0.257	27803
1000	0.75	0.6505	0.2449	0.732	0.917	-0.267	27978
Profit source B							
400	0.82	0.6882	0.1761	0.737	0.887	-0.199	29812
500	0.93	0.7141	0.1372	0.714	0.872	-0.157	29864
600	0.80	0.6944	0.1808	0.743	0.896	-0.202	29929
700	1.02	0.6469	0.1973	0.702	0.873	-0.226	29970
800	1.51	0.6529	0.1215	0.559	0.804	-0.151	30015
900	0.99	0.6728	0.1814	0.746	0.879	-0.206	30047
1000	0.78	0.7140	0.1728	0.778	0.905	-0.191	30070

Appendix D

Two-Firms and Asymmetric Taxation

This Appendix constructs a two-firm example to consider the effect on the time profile of aggregate taxable profits, and hence total corporation tax revenue, of the asymmetric treatment of losses in the tax structure. In particular, the way in which the elasticity of aggregate taxable profits with respect to gross profits varies over time when profits are subject to periods of below-trend growth followed by periods of above-trend growth. The way in which the corporation tax involves an asymmetry in the tax function, in that losses do not give rise to a tax rebate, was discussed above. Such losses they can be used during the period to offset positive profits from other sources within the corporation or across firms within a group of corporations defined for tax purposes, or carried forward to be used as tax offsets in future periods (where their use is more restricted).

Section D.1 demonstrates the potential complexity of the asymmetry for the analysis of changes over time. This complexity arises even in the very simplest of cases, that is where each firm has only one source of profit, and losses cannot be used as tax offsets across firms within a group. In view of this complexity, it is useful to examine some simple numerical examples. It is first necessary to specify a process describing the changing distribution of gross profits over time. This is the subject of Section D.2. Section D.3 considers the time profile of the elasticity of aggregate taxable profit with respect to gross profit, arising from periods of low and high growth relative to a trend value. The asymmetric treatment of losses is shown to give rise to an asymmetric elasticity cycle which becomes more asymmetric as the variation in profit growth around the trend increases.

D.1 Taxes and Losses

Consider a firm with total gross profit from all sources in period t of P_t. After various deductions, D_t, arising from capital allowances and losses (carried from previous periods, or current losses from sources within the firm or current losses of a group member, defined for tax purposes), the tax is a fixed proportion of taxable profit, $P^T = P_t - D_t$.[1] But this applies only for $P^T > 0$. Where losses are made, that is where $P_t < 0$ or where possible deductions are sufficient to make $P^T < 0$, there is no tax rebate. Any unused losses must either be used currently to offset profits in another firm in the group, or are carried forward to be used in future.[2]

The question considered here is how this asymmetry in the tax structure affects the time profile of the aggregate elasticity of P^T with respect to P, denoted $\eta_{P^T,P}$, where firms are subject to periods of relatively high growth followed by periods of relatively

---

[1] In the UK there is a lower rate applied over a very small range of taxable profits, but it is reasonable to consider a simple proportional tax here.

[2] When carried forward, losses can be used only against the profit source for which they arose, but current losses are much more flexible.

low growth rates. In the simple case where profit growth takes place at a constant, or trend, growth rate, (and there are no stochastic variations in growth rates of individual firms) this asymmetry has no, or a negligible, effect on the elasticity. Firms with positive profits continue (after exhausting any possible loss pools from earlier periods) to pay tax at a fixed proportional rate. Some firms which were previously making losses may move into positive profits in each year and can initially make use of their accumulated loss pools. However, with a large number of firms this latter effect is unlikely to influence the aggregate elasticity $\eta_{PT,P}$, and hence that of total revenue with respect to P. But if there are sustained periods of relatively low, or for some firms even negative, profit growth followed by sustained periods of above average growth, then the movement of firms into and out of losses is likely to be sufficient to affect the overall elasticity.

Examination of this issue is considerably complicated by the existence of multiple profit sources within corporations and the use of group relief of profits, in addition to the fact that profit offsets consist of losses and capital allowances. However, it turns out that the main characteristic of the profile of the elasticity, $\eta_{PT,P}$, over time is generated purely by the tax structure asymmetry. The additional, and considerable, complications associated with multiple profit sources and the use group relief merely modify, rather than cause, the characteristic. Hence, for present purposes this can be illustrated using a highly simplified framework.

Suppose that there is only one source of profit and that group relief is not allowed. Positive profits, P_t^+ are thus simply given by $P_t^+ = \max(P_t, 0)$ and losses are equal to $P_t^- = \max(-P_t, 0)$.

The loss pool, $L_{A,t}$, available for making deductions from P_t^+ is equal to current losses plus those carried over from the previous period, L_{t-1}, Hence $L_{A,t} = P_t^- + L_{t-1}$. Taxable profit is thus:

$$P_t^T = \max\left(P_t^+ - L_{A,t}, 0\right) \qquad (D.1)$$

and after making deductions, the loss pool to be carried to the next period is:

$$L_t = L_{A,t} - \min\left(P_t^+, L_{A,t}\right) \qquad (D.2)$$

Even with this highly simplified structure, it is far from clear how a convenient analytical expression might be obtained for the aggregate variation, over a distribution of firms, in taxable profit in relation to that of gross profit. The following discussion therefore uses numerical examples. It is first necessary to specify a process governing the growth of profits over time for the firms and this is described in the next section.

D.2   The Changing Distribution of Profits

The generation of changing profits over time cannot simply be a matter of applying a given growth rate to each firm's gross profit in each period, because it would lead loss-making firms to move further into losses during periods of above-trend growth.[3] The approach adopted here is to suppose that profit growth shifts the profit distribution upwards. Hence profits are converted into a positive variable, $x_{i,t}$, for form i where:

$$x_{i,t} = P_{i,t} + d_t \qquad (D.3)$$

---

[3]For example if the growth rate is 0.05, a firm with profit of 100 obtains 105 in the next period, whereas a firm with profit of -100 has a larger loss of -105.

and the parameter, d_t, is the maximum possible loss. This ensures that all values of x are positive. Profit growth therefore involves the application of a given growth rate, of say, $\dot{x}_t$, to all values of $x_{i,t}$. The time subscript on $\dot{x}$ allows growth of profits to vary in some way over time. Thus:

$$x_{i,t} = x_{i,t-1} \left(1 + \dot{x}_t\right) \tag{D.4}$$

Similarly, the maximum loss also varies over time, increasing in periods of relatively low values of $\dot{x}_t$ and decreasing when $\dot{x}_t$ is high. For example, in a recession when profit growth is lower on average, maximum losses are likely to become larger. Thus:

$$d_t = d_{t-1} \left(1 + \dot{d}_t\right) \tag{D.5}$$

Suppose there is a trend rate of growth of g and that periods of relatively low and high growth are symmetrical, involving a deviation from this trend of Δ. For example, in periods of above-trend growth, $\dot{x}_t = g + \Delta$ and $\dot{d}_t = g - \Delta$.

In terms of gross profit, $P_{i,t}$, the process in (D.4) becomes:

$$P_{i,t} + d_t = (P_{i,t-1} + d_{t-1}) \left(1 + \dot{x}_t\right) \tag{D.6}$$

and rearrangement gives:

$$P_{i,t} = P_{i,t-1} \left(1 + \dot{x}_t\right) + d_{t-1} \left(\dot{x}_t - \dot{d}_t\right) \tag{D.7}$$

The above model does not imply that all profits grow at the same rate when they are growing above or below the trend rate, because:

$$\frac{P_t - P_{t-1}}{P_{t-1}} = \dot{x}_t + \frac{d_{t-1}}{P_{t-1}} \left(\dot{x}_t - \dot{d}_t\right) \tag{D.8}$$

Along the trend path, $\dot{x}_t = \dot{x} = \dot{d}_t = \dot{d} = g$ for all t, $\dot{x}_t - \dot{d}_t = 0$ and indeed all firms' profits grow at $\dot{x}_t = g$. However, this does not hold for above- or below-trend growth. During high-growth periods $\dot{x}_t - \dot{d}_t = 2\Delta$ whereas for low-growth periods, $\dot{x}_t - \dot{d}_t = -2\Delta$. For large profit makers the term $d_{t-1}/P_{i,t-1}$ is low and hence the growth rate of profits is similar for all such firms at $\dot{x}_t$. However, for loss-makers, $-1 < d_{t-1}/P_{i,t-1} < \infty$. For the largest loss makers $d_{t-1}/P_{i,t-1}$ is close to -1 and the growth rate of profits is close to $\dot{d}_t$, so that bigger losses are made.

D.3   Numerical Examples

This section presents numerical examples of gross and taxable profit growth over alternating periods of low and high growth relative to a trend, using just two firms. One of the firms represents continuous profit makers, whereas the other firm, representing relatively small corporations, is assumed to begin with small positive profits and to turn to making losses (negative profits) during periods of below-trend growth.

Suppose the initial gross profit levels of the two firms are $P_{1,1} = 80$ $P_{2,1} = 3$, and that they begin in period 1 with no loss pools, so that $L_{1,1} = L_{2,1} = 0$. The maximum loss in period 1 is $d_1 = 80$. The two firms are then subject to the growth process described above. There is a trend rate of growth of $g = 0.005$, but a 'low growth' period, up to period 4, reduces growth below this value, so that $\dot{x}_t = 0.005 - \Delta$ for $t = 1, ..., 4$. From period 5 onwards there is a 'high growth' period where $\dot{x}_t = 0.005 + \Delta$ for $t = 5, ..., 10$. Table D.1 shows the resulting gross and net profit levels of each firm, the corresponding aggregate growth rates and the consequent elasticity $\eta_{P^T,P}$ (which is also equal to $\eta_{T,P}$ as the tax is proportional to P^T), for a range of values

Table D.1: Gross and Net Profits Over Time

t	2	3	4	5	6	7	8	9
Trend: $\dot{x} = \dot{d} = 0.005$								
P_1	80.40	80.80	81.21	81.61	82.02	82.43	82.84	83.26
P_2	3.01	3.03	3.05	3.06	3.08	3.09	3.11	3.12
Deviation from trend: $\Delta = 0.007$								
P_1	78.72	77.43	76.13	78.20	80.30	82.42	84.56	86.73
P_2	1.87	0.74	-0.41	0.74	1.91	3.09	4.28	5.48
P_2^T	1.87	0.74	0	0.33	1.91	3.09	4.28	5.48
$\dot{P}$	-0.029	-0.030	-0.031	0.043	0.041	0.040	0.039	0.038
$\dot{P}^T$	-0.029	-0.030	-0.026	0.032	0.047	0.040	0.039	0.038
$\eta_{P^T,P}$	1.0	1.0	0.832	0.741	1.132	1.0	1.0	1.0
Deviation from trend: $\Delta = 0.008$								
P_1	78.48	76.95	75.40	77.71	80.05	82.41	84.80	87.22
P_2	1.71	0.41	-0.91	0.41	1.75	3.09	4.45	5.82
P_2^T	1.71	0.41	0	0	1.25	3.09	4.45	5.82
$\dot{P}$	-0.034	-0.035	-0.037	0.049	0.047	0.045	0.044	0.042
$\dot{P}^T$	-0.034	-0.035	-0.025	0.031	0.046	0.052	0.044	0.042
$\eta_{P^T,P}$	1.0	1.0	0.683	0.629	0.984	1.140	1.0	1.0
Deviation from trend: $\Delta = 0.009$								
P_1	78.24	76.47	74.68	77.23	79.80	82.41	85.05	87.72
P_2	1.55	0.08	-1.40	0.08	1.58	3.09	4.62	6.16
P_2^T	1.55	0.08	0	0	0.26	3.09	4.62	6.16
$\dot{P}$	-0.039	-0.041	-0.043	0.055	0.053	0.051	0.049	0.047
$\dot{P}^T$	-0.039	-0.041	-0.024	0.034	0.037	0.068	0.049	0.047
$\eta_{P^T,P}$	1.0	1.0	0.572	0.620	0.698	1.341	1.0	1.0
Deviation from trend: $\Delta = 0.01$								
P_1	78.00	75.99	73.96	76.74	79.56	82.41	85.29	88.21
P_2	1.39	-0.25	-1.89	-0.25	1.41	3.09	4.78	6.50
P_2^T	1.39	0	0	0	0	2.11	4.78	6.50
$\dot{P}$	-0.044	-0.046	-0.049	0.061	0.059	0.056	0.054	0.051
$\dot{P}^T$	-0.044	-0.043	-0.027	0.038	0.037	0.062	0.066	0.051
$\eta_{P^T,P}$	1.0	0.933	0.550	0.612	0.627	1.116	1.227	1.000

of Δ. As firm 1 always has $P_{1,t} > 0$, then $P_{1,t}^T = P_{1,t}$ for all t and only gross profit needs to be reported. Values for period 1 are not shown as these are clearly the same for all cases. The first segment of the table gives, for comparison, the profit levels where $\Delta = 0$ and growth is constant at the trend value: in this case there are no losses and all gross and net profits grow by 0.005 and the elasticity, $\eta_{P^T,P}$, is always unity.

Consider the second segment relating to $\Delta = 0.007$. In this case firm 2 makes a loss in period 4 of 0.41. In view of the asymmetry of the tax structure this loss does not give rise to a rebate but is used in period 5 to reduce the gross profit of 0.74 to 0.33. This has two effects. First, the subsequent growth in period 6 of P^T is higher than otherwise, since the base is lower: the effect of this is to produce an elasticity $\eta_{P^T,P}$ that is greater than 1 in period 6. However, this effect lasts only one period and the elasticity quickly settles to unity for the remaining high-growth periods. Second, during period 4 when firm 2 makes a loss the aggregate taxable profit is simply that of firm 1, and in period 5 the growth of taxable profit is also lower than that of gross profit because of the use of the loss pool inherited from the earlier period. Hence the low growth period results in two periods when the elasticity, $\eta_{P^T,P}$, is less than 1. The combined effect is that the asymmetric treatment of losses in the tax structure leads to an asymmetry in the time profile of $\eta_{P^T,P}$ over low- and high-growth periods. During periods of low growth the elasticity becomes less than 1 for much of the time, and this extends into the early high-growth periods while loss pools are being used. During periods of relatively high growth, the elasticity is unity after loss pools are exhausted, except for a short overshoot when it exceeds unity.

As the value of Δ increases, the number of periods during which firm 2 makes a loss increases, the absolute size of the losses increases, and thus the loss pool built up for later use, when firm 2 moves into positive profits, is larger. Hence the losses are not exhausted in the first period of above-trend growth. This means that the period when $\eta_{PT,P} > 1$ is delayed until later. For example, when $\Delta = 0.008$, even though firm 2 continues to make a loss in period 4 only, the loss of 0.91 is not exhausted in period 5, so that 0.50 is available in period 6 to reduce taxable profit. Hence the period of maximum $\eta_{PT,P}$ is period 6. When the deviation from trend is larger, at $\Delta = 0.01$, losses are made by firm 2 in periods 2, 3 and 4 and a loss pool of 2.39 is available in period 6. Only 1.41 of this is needed to reduce taxable profit to zero, leaving a further 0.98 for period 7, allowing taxable profit to be reduced in that period to 2.11, from a gross profit of 3.09. Hence the period of maximum $\eta_{PT,P}$ is pushed to period 8. If the deviations from trend growth were smoother – for example if $\dot{x}_t$ and $\dot{d}_t$ were to follow a sine wave – loss-making firms would move into positive profit much earlier during the phase of above-trend growth and the elasticity $\eta_{PT,P}$ would return to unity earlier.

Importantly, the deeper losses arising as Δ increases also mean that during the low-growth periods, when both gross and taxable profits fall, aggregate gross profit falls much faster than aggregate taxable profit while firm 2 makes losses. The fall in taxable profit is determined purely by the positive gross profits of firm 1 while the fall in gross profit is influenced by the deeper losses of firm 2. The implication of this is that $\eta_{PT,P}$ is not only less than 1 but also becomes smaller as Δ increases. Hence the asymmetry in the behaviour of $\eta_{PT,P}$ over low- and high-growth periods becomes more pronounced as Δ increases: Table D.1 shows that the minimum elasticity falls gradually from 0.741 when $\Delta = 0.007$ to 0.550 when $\Delta = 0.01$. The fact that loss pools built up during the low-growth phase are not immediately exhausted when firm 2 begins to make positive gross profit, as discussed in the previous paragraph, also means that the increasing asymmetry involves not just a deeper effect on $\eta_{PT,P}$ but a longer period during which it lies below unity.

Bibliography

[1] Agúndez, A. (2006). The delineation and apportionment of an EU consolidated tax base for multi-jurisdictional corporate income taxation: a review of issues and options. *European Commission Working Paper No. 9.*

[2] Altshuler, R. and Auerbach, A.J. (1990) The significance of tax law asymmetries: an empirical investigation. *Quarterly Journal of Economics*, 105, pp. 61-86.

[3] Auerbach, A.J. (1986) The dynamic effects of tax law asymmetries. *Review of Economic Studies*, 53, pp. 205-225.

[4] Auerbach, A.J. (2002)Taxation and Corporate Financial Policy. In *Handbook of Public Economics*, Vol. 3 (ed. by A.J. Auerbach and M. Feldstein), pp. 1251-1292. New York: Elsevier.

[5] Auerbach, A.J. (2007) Why have corporation tax revenues declined? Another look. *CESifo Economic Studies*, pp. 1-19.

[6] Auerbach, A.J. and Poterba, J.M. (1987) Why have corporate tax revenues declined? In *Tax Policy and the Economy* (ed. by L. Summers), pp. 1-28. Cambridge: MIT Press.

[7] Bakker, A. and Creedy, J. (1999) Macroeconomic variables and income inequality in New Zealand: an exploration using conditional mixture distributions. *New Zealand Economic Papers*, 33, pp. 59-79.

[8] Bartelsman, E.J. and Beetsma, R.M.W.J. (2003) Why pay more? Corporate tax avoidance through transfer pricing in OECD countries. *Journal of Public Economics*, 87, pp. 2225-2252.

[9] Carroll, R. and Hrung, W. (2005) What does the taxable income elasticity say about dynamic responses to tax changes. *American Economic Review*, 95, pp. 426-431.

[10] Clausing, K.A. (2007) Corporate tax revenues in OECD countries. *International Tax and Public Finance*, 14, pp. 115-133.

[11] Clausing, K.A. (2009) Multinational firm tax avoidance and tax policy. *National Tax Journal*, 62, pp. 703-725.

[12] Cooper, M. and Knittel, M (2006) Partial loss refundability: how are corporate tax losses used? *National Tax Journal*, 59, pp. 651-663.

[13] Creedy, J. (2009) The elasticity of taxable income: an introduction. *University of Melbourne Department of Economics Working Paper*.

[14] Creedy, J. (1998) *The Dynamics of Inequality and Poverty: Comparing Income Distributions*. Cheltenham: Edward Elgar.

[15] Creedy, J. and Gemmell, N. (2006) *Modelling Tax Revenue Growth.* Cheltenham: Edward Elgar.

[16] Creedy, J. and Gemmell, N. (2008) Corporation tax buoyancy and revenue elasticity in the UK. *Economic Modelling,* 25, pp. 24-37.

[17] Creedy, J. and Gemmell, N. (2009) Corporation tax revenue growth in the UK: a microsimulation analysis. *Economic Modelling,* 26, pp. 614-625.

[18] Creedy, J. and Gemmell, N. (2010a) Modelling responses to profit taxation over the economic cycle: the case of the UK corporation tax. *FinanzArchiv* (forthcoming).

[19] Creedy, J. and Gemmell, N. (2010b) Behavioural responses to corporate profit taxation. *Hacienda Pública Española,* 193, pp. 109-130.

[20] Creedy, J. and Gemmell, N. (2010c) Corporation tax asymmetries: effective tax rates and profit shifting. *International Tax and Public Finance* (forthcoming).

[21] Demirgüç-Kunt, A. and Huizinga, H. 2001, The taxation of domestic and foreign banking. *Journal of Public Economics,* 79, pp. 429-453.

[22] Devereux, M.P. (1989) Tax asymmetries, the cost of capital and investment: some evidence from United Kingdon panel data. *Economic Journal,* 99, pp. 103-112.

[23] Devereux, M.P. (2008) Corporation Tax: Trends, Principles and Feasibility. Presentation to OECD Committee for Fiscal Affairs, Paris.

[24] Devereux, M.P. and Hubbard, R.G. (2003) Taxing multinationals. *International Tax and Public Finance*, 10, pp. 469-487.

[25] Devereux, M.P. and Sorensen, P.B. (2005) The corporate income tax: international trends and options for fundamental reform. *University of Copenhagen Economic Policy Research Unit Working Paper*, no. 2005/24.

[26] Devereux, M.P., Griffith, R. and Klemm, A (2004) How has the UK corporation tax raised so much revenue? *Fiscal Studies*, 25, pp. 367-388.

[27] Devereux, M.P., Lockwood, B. and Redoano, M. (2008) Do countries compete over corporate tax rates? *Journal of Public Economics*, 92, pp. 1210-1235.

[28] Dischinger, M. (2007) Profit shifting by multinationals: indirect evidence from European micro data. *University of Munich Department of Economics Discussion Paper*, 2007-30.

[29] Donnelly, M. and Young, A. (2002) Policy options for tax loss treatment: how does Canada compare? *Canadian Tax Journal*, 50, 429-488.

[30] Dwenger, N.and Steiner, V. (2008) Effective profit taxation and the elasticity of the corporate income tax base: evidence from German corporate tax return data. *German Institute for Economic Research, Berlin, Working Paper*, no. 829.

[31] Edgerton, J. (2007) Investment Incentives and Corporate tax Asymmetries. Unpublished manuscript, MIT.

[32] Feldstein, M. (1995) The effect of marginal tax rates on taxable income. A panel study of the 1986 tax reform act. *Journal of Political Economy*, 103, pp. 551-572.

[33] Feldstein, M. (1999) Tax avoidance and the deadwight loss of the income tax. *Review of Economics and Statistics*, 81, pp. 674-680.

[34] Feldstein, M., Hines, J.R. and Hubbard, R.G. (eds) (1995) *The Effects of Taxation on Multinational Corporations*. Chicago: Chicago University Press.

[35] Gordon, R.H. and Slemrod, J. (1998) Are 'real' responses to taxes simply income shifting between corporate and personal tax bases? *National Bureau of Economic Reseach Working Paper*, no. 6576.

[36] Gresik, T.A. (2001) The taxing task of taxing multinationals. *Journal of Economic Literature*, 39, pp. 800-838.

[37] Gruber, J. and Saez, E. (2002) The elasticity of taxable income: evidence and implications. *Journal of Public Economics*, 84, pp. 1-32.

[38] Grubert, H. (2003) Intangible income, intercompany transactions, income shifting, and the choice of location. *National Tax Journal*, 56, p. 221-242.

[39] Grubert, H. and Mutti, J. (1991) Taxes, tariffs and transfer pricing in multinational corporate decision making. *Review of Economics and Statistics*, 75, pp. 285-293.

[40] Grubert, H. and Slemrod, J. (1998) The effect of taxes on investment and income shifting to Puerto Rico. *Review of Economics and Statistics*, 80, pp. 365-373.

[41] Harris, D.G. (1993) The impact of U.S. tax law revision on multinational corporations' capital location and income shifting, *Journal of Accounting Research*, 31, pp. 111-140.

[42] Heinemann, F. (2001) After the death of inflation: will fiscal drag survive? *Fiscal Studies*, 22, pp. 527-546.

[43] Hines, J.R. (1999) Lessons from behavioural responses to international taxation. *National Tax Journal*, 52, pp. 305-322.

[44] Hines, J.R. and Rice, E.M. (1994) Fiscal paradise: foreign tax havens and American business. *Quarterly Journal of Economics*, 109, pp. 149-182.

[45] Huizinga, H. and Laeven, L. (2007) International profit shifting within European Multinationals. *CEPR Dicussion Paper*, No. 6048.

[46] Kemsley, D. (1998) The effect of taxes on production location. *Journal of Accounting Research*, 36, pp. 321-341.

[47] Klemm, A. and McCrae, J. (2002) Reform of corporation tax: a response to the government's consultation document. *Institute for Fiscal Studies Briefing Note BN30*.

[48] Markusen, J.R. (2002) *Multinational Firms and the Theory of International Trade*. Cambridge, Mass.: MIT Press.

[49] Metz, R. and Weale, M. (2003) Modelling corporation tax. (Unpublished paper). London: National Institute of Economic and Social Research.

[50] Myers, S.C. and Majd, S. (1986) Tax asymmetries and corporate income tax reform. *National Bureau of Economic Research Working Paper*, 1779-86.

[51] National Statistics (2005) *The United Kingdom National Accounts*. The Blue Book. Basingstoke: Palgrave Macmillan.

[52] Office of Tax Policy (2007) Approaches to improve the competitiveness of the US business tax system for the 21st century. Washington, DC: Office of Tax Policy, US Department of the Treasury.

[53] Saez, E., Slemrod, J.B. and Giertz, S.H. (2009) The elasticity of taxable income with respect to marginal tax rates: a critical review. *National Bureau of Economic Research Working Paper*, no. 15012.

[54] Slemrod, J. (1995) Income creation of income shifting? Behavioural responses to the Tax Reform Act of 1986. *American Economic Review Papers and Proceedings*, 85, pp. 175-180.

[55] Slemrod, J and Yitzhaki, S. (2002) Tax avoidance, evasion, and administration. In *Handbook of Public Economics Volume 3*. (edited by A.J. Auerback and M. Feldstein), pp. 1423-1470. Amsterdam: Elsevier.

Index